The Swiss Cheese Theory of Life!

How to Get Through Life's Holes Without Getting Stuck in Them!

Judith A. Belmont, MS
Lora Shor, LSW

Library of Congress Cataloging-in-Publication Data

Belmont, Judith.

The swiss cheese theory of life / Judith Belmont, Lora Shor. p. cm.

ISBN 978-0-9820398-9-2 (pbk.) -- ISBN 978-1-936128-03-7 (hardcover) 1. Resilience (Personality trait) 2. Life skills. 3. Survival skills. I. Shor, Lora. II. Title.

BF698.35.R47B45 2010

158.1--dc22

2010047443

www.pesi.com

This book shows you how to take complete control of your thoughts and emotions, and live a wonderful life!

Brian Tracy
International Motivational Speaker and Author of *No Excuses! The Power of Self-Discipline*

An engagingly fun "cookbook" of recipes for self-discovery. Tips, tests, tool-kits, and clever insights make for a practical handbook for harnessing your emotions and fulfilling your life-goals.

Neal Roese, Ph.D.
Northwestern University, Kellogg School of Management
Author of *If Only: How To Turn Regret Into Opportunity*

In today's complicated and challenging society, we often struggle to make sense of the bad hand that life sometimes deals us. *The Swiss Cheese Theory of Life* offers a simple, yet compelling guide to follow in achieving personal transformation. This book offers a refreshing approach to helping us 'reshuffle the deck' and tap into that inner resilience that we need to achieve a more fruitful existence. I highly recommend this book to anyone who is contemplating changing their life.

Frank M. Dattilio, Ph.D., ABPP
Author and Editor
Department of Psychiatry, Harvard Medical School

Even if you are lactose intolerant *The Swiss Cheese Theory of life*, will offer you some really valuable advice to help you get through difficult times and live life in a balanced way.

Sophie Keller
Happiness Expert and Author of *How Happy Is* book series

Smart, concise and clever, *The Swiss Cheese Theory of Life* offers brief therapy for dealing with disappointment, loss and leftovers from a dysfunctional childhood.

Jane Adams, Ph.D.
Author, *Boundary Issues* and *I'm Still Your Mother*

Although therapy is one of the greatest gifts to humanity, it is still under-utilized due to stigma and costs. Judy Belmont and Lora Shor see this obstacle as just another hole in the Swiss Cheese to get through. They get through it with this very charming, fun and informative book. They use the Swiss Cheese metaphor to show you how to get unstuck from just about any stressful situation. They have taken some of the most effective therapeutic tools and they offer it up in a delicious fondue of wisdom for everyone to enjoy. I highly recommend it.

Robert M. Gordon, Ph.D., ABPP
Author, *An Expert Look at Love, Intimacy and Personal Growth.*
Board Certified in Clinical Psychology and
Psychoanalysis in Psychology
The Institute for Advanced Psychological Training

Using a humorous, lighthearted touch, Belmont and Shor provide a clear analysis of what so often goes wrong, and perspectives on getting through life's rough spots. Buy one to enjoy on your own, and copies for your friends who are always complaining!

Shel Horowitz
Best-selling primary author of *Guerrilla Marketing Goes Green*

With the pace of change at unprecedented levels, every corporate leader will profit from the field-tested practical and fun wisdom contained in this book. Given how many businesses are totally up in the air when it comes to knowing what to do next, it's time to pay attention to what the "holes" in your business have to teach you and how to manage your way through them! This book shows you how.

Dave Laveman
Founding Partner Emeritus
Praemia Group - Global Leadership Consulting

...filled with delectable tidbits on how to stay centered, patient and tolerant as we live with the complexities and pace of our world today...

Dee Slavutin, President
Stern Slavutin - 2 Inc.
Wealth Management, Financial and Estate Planning

Acknowledgments

From Judy Belmont

This book was inspired by the numerous people who I have worked with through the years in my various roles as therapist, speaker, educator and trainer. Individuals who have shown confidence in me by opening up their hearts and minds have taught me so much about human strength and resilience, and getting to work with them has provided the insight that has been the foundation for this book.

I am grateful most of all for Don, who has given me the love, support and encouragement all these years that has provided the foundation for a wonderful life. He has been an excellent role model for emotional strength and resiliency. My special gratitude also extends to Justin, Brian and Adam for making my life such a fascinating adventure, and giving me the opportunity to be such a proud mom! I appreciate my dad's resilient mindset, as well as his unconditional love. I have been blessed with so many wonderful friends and family members and their support and friendship has meant so much to me. This network of great people has provided a support system that has made my life so much more special just because they are in it.

Of course, this book would not have been possible without Lora, as it is our collaboration that resulted in a book that combines the best of our knowledge and insights. A chance meeting, many years ago at a mindfulness seminar, proved to open up a path to friendship, collaboration and synergy, which resulted in *The Swiss Cheese Theory of Life*. The concept of this book came to life as a result of our like-mindedness, zest for humor and creativity, as well as our passion for helping others develop practical tools for personal empowerment and resiliency. The direction and success of this book lies in this collaborative effort; and her infectious love of humor and laughter has made the journey most enjoyable!

From Lora Shor

The writing of this book has been a wonderful experience for me. There have been many teachers and mentors whose guidance has helped throughout my life. I have had the opportunity to speak and listen to some of the most resourceful and interesting individuals throughout my career as a work/life consultant. Some of the greatest life lessons have come from my clients who have taught me that we can all learn by having an open mind.

I am grateful that I learned the value of perseverance which helped throughout my life in the face of adversity. There have been many tragic losses in my life–most of my family perished in the Holocaust, yet my mother and father had extreme courage and overcame tremendous obstacles. I learned so much about resilience from them, which helped to guide me throughout my life.

Thanks to all my wonderful friends whose love, laughter, time, wisdom and support keeps going strong. To my three children, Chad, Alix and Carly, for their unending love. We have all taught each other "how to really get through the holes in our lives." I admire our resilient nature, and treasure all our experiences and time together on this incredible journey. We always know that possibilities are endless when you believe in yourself, use your time and energy wisely, and have an attitude of gratitude.

This book would have never come to fruition without the fortuitous meeting that took place years ago at a mindfulness seminar. Judy and I connected, collaborated, and combined our talents to create this delightful and insightful book. She brought her rich knowledge, integrity, direction, values and team effort from beginning to end. It has been a pleasure to work with such a bright, talented person who has a great heart and shares my sense of humor (or at least laughs at my jokes).

From Both of Us

We both want to thank the dedicated and talented team at Premier Education Solutions, including our publishers, Darren Kirby, Mike Olson, and Linda Jackson. We are particularly grateful for Linda's steadfast patience, support and continued communication as we navigated the holes of publishing! We also appreciate the amazing talents of cover designer, Brianna Dunham; cartoon illustrator and graphic designer, Amy Wilder; Premier's in-house editor, Kayla Omtvedt; and our general editors, Sara Vigneri and Sarah Doyle. We also want to thank Randy Glasbergen, whose cartoons have helped make our work come alive in a way that we could have not done without his talent.

Judy and Lora

2011

About the Authors

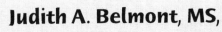

Judith A. Belmont, MS,

is a national speaker, corporate wellness trainer, member of the National Speakers Association, and a member of the Association for Journalists and Authors. With a B.S. in Psychology from The University of Pennsylvania and an M.S. in Clinical Psychology from Hahnemann Medical College, her experience as a psychotherapist and educator spans over 30 years. In her counseling practice, as well as in her role as consultant and speaker, her primary focus has been to offer practical strategies to others to improve personal empowerment and boost emotional resilience.

She is a national speaker and her seminars and keynotes are based on her zeal for life skills education, and the highlights of these ideas provide the basis of *The Swiss Cheese Theory of Life*. She is the author of two other books, *86 TIPS for the Therapeutic Toolbox* and *103 Group Activities and TIPS*, designed to offer mental health professionals and trainers practical guidance to coach emotional resiliency.

Judy has served as a mental health expert for various radio talk shows, TV interviews, and has been widely quoted in various on-line and print publications.

She is the Founder of Worksite Insights, which offers an array of Wellness seminars, coaching and consultation services to the workplace.

x

About the Authors

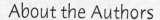

Lora Shor, MSW,

Lora Shor, MSW, LSW, is a work/life consultant to global corporations, health care systems, universities, employee assistance programs, financial and legal institutions, the stock exchange and The United States Government. She has written and presented hundreds of workshops and seminars for Fortune 500 companies including Wells Fargo/ Wachovia, Aetna, Pfizer, AmerisourceBergen, Air Products, United Health, Merck, Morgan Stanley, PG&E, Arrow International, and DuPont, among many others. These workshops cover topics such as balancing work and personal life, stress reduction, mindfulness and the positive power of change. She has helped thousands of people understand, learn and implement resiliency skills and techniques for a happier, healthier lifestyle. Lora creates and teaches CE courses and international corporate webinars. She earned a master's degree in clinical social work from The University of Southern California where she began her training in healthcare leadership teaching multidisciplinary teams effective communication skills.

Lora is a member of The National Speakers Association, and actively uses her incredibly contagious energy, enthusiasm and sense of humor to motivate and maximize personal potential and growth. These transformative life lessons have become part of *The Swiss Cheese Theory of Life*. This book, is designed to help all of us get through the "holes" in our life in a powerful, practical, playful and holistic way. Lora Shor is President of ForShor Wellness and she maintains a private practice in the Philadelphia area.

The **Ten** Digestible Slices of Life

> Enjoy these delectable, delicious
> and easily digestible slices of life
> ... Go ahead and have a taste!

The Swiss Cheese Theory of Life

In *The Swiss Cheese Theory of Life*, Swiss cheese is a metaphor for life itself. Swiss cheese *needs* holes to truly be Swiss. Without the characteristic holes, Swiss, as we know it, would not exist! As in life, it is the holes or imperfections that give us character. At times, the holes in our lives often appear huge, like craters, disrupting our life satisfaction and happiness. *Wouldn't it be nice if our lives were smooth and predictable like cream cheese?* It's human nature to believe, and even to expect, that our lives will go smoothly and turn out the way we hope. Yet at times, life leaves us unsettled, bitter and stuck in a hole. *The Swiss Cheese Theory of Life* helps us make peace with the disappointments and unrealized expectations. It helps us accept, manage and embrace the inevitable holes poked in our hopes and dreams. Through this insight, we build on our experiences to overcome life's obstacles and move through the holes with a new perspective. This is how we gain resiliency–the ability to spring back from life's challenges. Sure, some lives have more holes than others, and you might feel angry that you have more than your fair share. However, the amount and depth of the holes matters less than how you deal with them, and your resolve to move through them.

Life is FULL of holes.
How you get through them is what counts!

 You...and the
Cheese

Can Swiss cheese really be used as a valid metaphor for overcoming the challenges and adversities in our lives? *Undoubtedly, YES!* The holes in the Swiss are created through gassy bacteria and acidified milk. This process does not exactly elicit pleasant thoughts, but neither do the obstacles in our lives! The wonder of this process is that the flavor, texture and sweetness of the cheese emerge from bacteria and acid. Just as the darkness of the night yields to the lightness of the dawn and dark soil provides the foundation for beautiful flowers, it is from our challenges in life that we emerge and experience new growth. As we move through the holes in our lives to get through to the other side, we gain meaning, purpose, strength and character.

To take the analogy further:
Here's a secret that only cheese makers know:
The larger the holes, the sweeter the cheese!
In fact, it is the cheese maker's art to create larger holes by fermenting the bacteria. That's right! Specialty cheese makers carefully ferment the cheese to make bigger holes. So it is the larger holes that make the cheese more flavorful!

Applying this analogy to life, we can emerge from the difficult times in our lives, *the moments that seem laden with bacteria,* to taste life's sweetness!

So let's bite into the slices of
The Swiss Cheese Theory of Life!

Q: Have you ever asked yourself: "What would Swiss be without the holes?"

A: If you are like most people, the answer is "NO"! We accept Swiss cheese as it is. We do not critique it. We do not judge that its holes are too big, too small, too numerous, or in the wrong place. We do not find fault with the Swiss, wishing that it would be more like Gouda, Fontina, or Roquefort. We love its individuality and distinctiveness, and wouldn't want it to be anything else!

In short, we enjoy Swiss cheese with all its imperfections. Swiss just "is."

If we could only accept LIFE like that!

Truly, if we could apply this concept to *important* stuff, like the events in our lives, we would be so much happier! It is so common to be taken aback and even immobilized by the obstacles and imperfections of day-to-day living. Many of us struggle with events which have spun out of control.

Sometimes life throws you a huge curve ball, leading to disappointment and anger. Sure, it would be nice to have things go your way, but we are not always on the winning team. Sometimes we win, sometimes we tie, and sometimes we lose. Some people really do get better breaks!

Are you stuck in why-does-this-happen-to-me thinking?

Do you spend too much time protesting against the unfairness and inequality of life?

Do you spend more time waiting for things to smooth out rather than trying to make them work out?

Which do you prefer, Bleu or Swiss cheese?

Dwelling on unfulfilled dreams leaves us feeling blue, like moldy bleu cheese. We end up more like Roquefort than Swiss! Undoubtedly, there is a time and a place to linger in the hole to develop a game plan to overcome obstacles and emerge on the other side stronger and wiser. Just don't hang out there too long! Too much wishing and hoping leads you through a maze of delayed disappointment, at best, and emotional distress and disturbance, at worst.

Client Example:
Pulling a Low Card

Does it seem at times that other people's lives are so exquisitely smooth like American, while you are slogging through the potholes of Swiss? If you compare yourself to others, you'll often come up short.

From her first appointment, Lisa seemed nervous and carried herself with little confidence. She confided that when she compared herself to others, she felt inadequate.

In counseling, she learned to accept herself rather than measure herself constantly against others who appeared to be more worthy. Once she stopped measuring her self-worth based on how she compared herself with others, she got to work on being a *victor* and not a *victim*.

During one session, I pulled out a deck of playing cards and asked her to pick one; she drew an eight. I reminded her that despite the fact it is not as high as the royal cards, and perhaps not as impressive, it sometimes is the best card. For example, if she had picked the eight in the game Crazy Eights, it would be better than any other card, even though it would be nothing special in any other card game. How about a two, the lowest of the low? If she were playing Deuces Wild, she would have it made! This analogy showed her that it is not the cards you are dealt, but the meaning you give to them, and how you play the hand. Wishing that you had other cards and getting angry that you don't prevents you from playing the cards you have!

If you find yourself wishing that you were dealt other cards in life, shift your focus to playing the hand that you were dealt instead of wishing things were different!

Why can't my life be smoother, like cream cheese, instead of being like holey Swiss?

That is like saying:

- I try to be such a good person—why do people give me such grief?

- My sister's children are so gifted; my kids should be more like them!

- He is much more successful than I am–if I had just made other career decisions, I could have been just as successful as him!

- I would be so much happier if I was thin and attractive like my next door neighbor. She doesn't even have to work at it!

"Flamingos have thin thighs, but they don't seem any happier than you."

NOTE: *Don't look around at others and envy what they do, for they too, look at someone, and someone looks at you.*

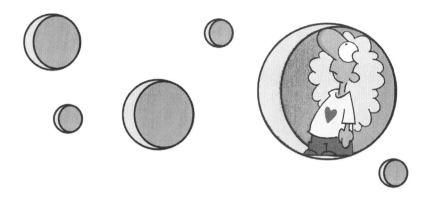

Do you feel Hol(e)y?

By now we think you've gotten the point that without the holes, we would not be:

(W)hole *and we would not be* Hol(e)y!

What are people like who embrace life's holes?

They are the people who:

- Accept themselves as a package deal, blemishes and all!
- Are able to examine themselves and feel at peace.
- Are aware of their surroundings and do not have tunnel vision.
- Embrace their self-worth without question.
- See their shortcomings and still like themselves.
- Love themselves and others without preconditions.
- View successes and failures as all part of the journey.
- Do not wait for things to come together someday. They choose to work on making things come together TODAY!

Consider this!

Technically, according to cheese makers, the
holes in Swiss cheese are called eyes. Likewise, it
is the holes in our lives that allow us to *see* more clearly!

> It is true that there are some forms of Swiss cheese without any holes
> at all. This type of Swiss is called Blind Swiss. What an analogy to
> life itself! It is unhealthy to ignore life's holes or wish them away.
> They are real, and make us who we are! When you live your life
> without insight and do not look beyond the obvious, you are living
> like Blind Swiss. *You might consider that cheese in denial!*

If you want to open up to life, don't close your eyes! If you want to
experience life, you need eyes as much as you need the holes! Our eyes
offer us a chance to develop insight, and might even be the secrets to
success. Consider the following *eyes:*

- In the game of archery, darts or riflery, winning requires hitting
  the bull's-*eye!*

- New sprouts grow through the *eyes* of the potato.

- How about the *eye* of the needle? Without the thread going
  through the hole, you would not be able to sew!

- It is through the *eye* of the camera lens that we are able to capture
  life's beauty!

Are you ready to see things through new eyes?

Consider this too!

The human body exemplifies the importance of holes. We have holes throughout our bodies and we need them to function!

It is the holes in our body that allow us to:

- *Breathe...*Without breath there is no life.

- *Sweat...*We use sweat to cool down!

- *Procreate...*Make love, not war!

- *See...*Open your eyes to the wonder that is around you.

- *Hear...*Listen to the sweet sound of music.

- *Smell...*Take time to smell the roses!

- *Eat...*Sample the delectable slices of life!

- *Drink...*Hydrate your body!

- *Eliminate...*The body removes toxins as waste!

*So as you can see, holes are
everywhere—and we need them to live!*

Looking at the Bright Side of the Holes in Swiss Cheese...and Life!

- The more holes, the fewer the calories.

- Just as we seek lightness in our lives, the holes of the cheese let the air and light come in!

- The larger the holes, the sweeter and more flavorful the cheese.

- It is the holes of the Swiss that make it look so distinctive and appealing!

- Life's holes and obstacles offer us the opportunity to overcome adversity.

- Getting through the holes builds our character and resilience.

- It is often the unexpected holes which offer the greatest possibilities for growth!

The holes of the Swiss add a sense of distinctiveness to the cheese, and your life will be more distinctive the more successfully you navigate life's holes. Playing it safe can get stale!

Life is fine when it is even and predictable–
like vanilla ice cream. But wouldn't you like to
add some sprinkles and nuts to give it some

PIZZAZZ?

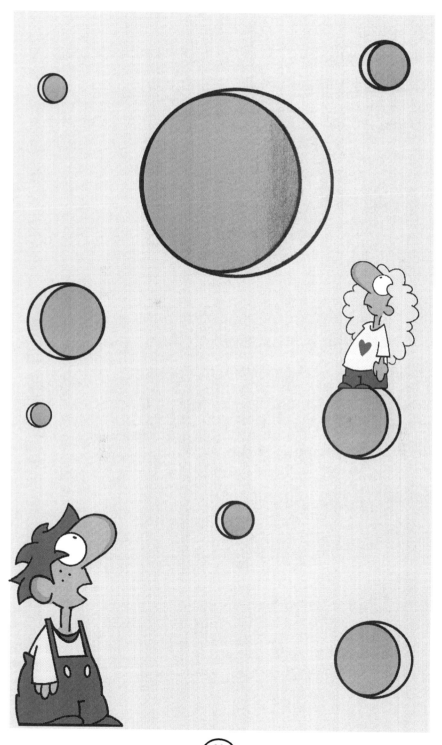

Introducing our Guides–Getting a Taste of the Swiss

The Swiss Wiz
In life, the value of having mentors, teachers and coaches cannot be overestimated. Consider the Swiss Wiz your very own personal mentor who will guide you through the slices of life's lessons. Throughout the book, he will teach you the ten important slices of wisdom that will get you through life's obstacles. The Wiz does not avoid, pretend, deny or wish the holes away. He does not get upset that the holes ruin the smoothness of the cheese, and he does not spend time thinking of reasons why it is unfair. Rather, he crystallizes the profound truths that Swiss cheese can teach us, offering slices of wisdom that help us successfully navigate the holes in our lives rather than get stuck in them.

The Swiss Cheese Fairy of Life
The Swiss Cheese Fairy of Life will complement the Wizard's teachings by offering uplifting affirmations and nurturing reminders. She sprinkles fairy dust, much like Parmesan cheese, to help you find your inner strength and magic within. Similar to The Good Witch in *The Wizard of Oz*, who helped Dorothy and her friends find the answers to their dilemmas, The Swiss Cheese Fairy will help you find the answers within yourself. She will help you peel away layers to find your inner strength. She understands the importance of self-love and self-acceptance. She loves you and teaches you how to love yourself.

The Stinky Cheese
The Stinky Cheese represents unhealthy thought habits and self-sabotaging self-talk. In times of stress, the Stinky Cheese reacts with negative, rigid, bitter and distorted thoughts and does not have the awareness that this way of thinking is a choice. He doesn't realize that things will never change without a major attitude adjustment. *The Stinky Cheese is a true pessimist.* When he looks at a doughnut, he sees only the emptiness of the hole. The Stinky Cheese will not cut you a break, and will bring you down rather than build you up.

The Swiss Wiz

The Swiss Cheese Fairy of Life

The Stinky Cheese

Do you remember Goofus and Gallant from Highlights© magazine for children? Goofus showed the wrong way to do something–the unhealthy way–and Gallant showed us the healthier alternative—the dos, not the don'ts.

The Swiss Cheese Fairy and The Swiss Wiz represent Gallant. They are validating and wise, as opposed to The Stinky Cheese, who shows us only negativity and self-sabotaging thoughts and behavior. The Swiss Cheese Fairy and The Swiss Wiz will guide you through the maze of the ten digestible slices of *The Swiss Cheese Theory of Life*. In contrast, The Stinky Cheese will show you how things can go wrong when you let negativity and judgmental thoughts pervade your way of thinking.

Who are you most like?

In the words of

The Swiss Wiz...

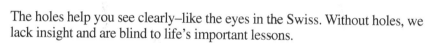

It's a fact! The larger the holes, the sweeter the cheese! If Swiss is like that, why can't life be like that too?

Remember, it is the acidic process that gives the cheese its distinctive flavor! As we often see in life, it is the most difficult times that yield the greatest opportunity to build character.

The holes help you see clearly–like the eyes in the Swiss. Without holes, we lack insight and are blind to life's important lessons.

In the words of

The Swiss Cheese Fairy of Life...

I will serve as your guide to learn to accept and love yourself, imperfections and all.

You are a gift to the world! You are special!

To make peace with life's holes, first make peace with yourself and embrace who you are.

Your uniqueness comes from just being you. You are worthy exactly as you are.

Swiss Cheese
Tool Kit

Assembling the Metaphorical Tool Kit

In every slice of *The Swiss Cheese Theory of Life* we invite you to imagine, or even literally assemble, a Swiss Cheese Tool Kit. The main lesson from each chapter will be represented by familiar items, each symbolizing one of the ten important concepts outlined. You can use something as simple as a medium-size clear plastic bag to hold the ten items, one from each of our slices of life. After finishing the book and assembling your bag with the symbolic contents, you might keep it in a place tucked away for times when you feel like you need to recall what *The Swiss Cheese Theory of Life* slices can teach you. Or you might want to keep it in a prominent place to serve as a daily reminder of the important life skills/lessons that this toolkit offers.

The Ten Digestible Slices of Life
...According to the Swiss Wiz

How to get through the holes...
without getting stuck in them!

First Slice

Fondue Can Never Turn Back Into a Block of Cheese

Giving up the Habit ... of Regret

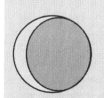

Fondue Can Never Turn Back Into a Block of Cheese!
Giving up the Habit...of Regret

Do you find yourself focusing too often on the past?

Do you have thoughts starting with 'If only' or 'I should have known'?

Do you find that you spend too much time reworking past decisions that cannot be changed?

Do you carry an emotional backpack that weighs you down with too many woulda, coulda, shouldas?

If you're like most people, the answer is a resounding YES to many of the above. There are many directions to choose from in the maze of life. There are many roads not taken, which gives plenty of opportunities for *what-if* thinking. Sometimes the paths we choose seem to end up like dead ends. The lessons learned from roads taken, or not taken, provide information to transform your today. Build on your *woulda, coulda, shouldas!*–use every day as a chance to rewrite your destiny. Many times in life we get to try again. Just consider the game of bowling–you get a second chance in each frame! If things do not work out like you hoped in the first frame, you get another try. While there are few do overs in life, there are second chances!

What Lessons
Have You Learned?

In the popular Carrie Underwood song, *Lessons Learned*, regret is featured prominently as a source of pain, but it also offers a potential source of wisdom over lessons learned.

The past is a great place to visit, but you don't want to live there! The past can truly be a very enticing place to go, but don't linger too long. Rather than getting stuck, use the lessons learned to move forward.

Ask the Therapist

Q: Why is it so tempting (with the benefit of hindsight), to use the past as a hitching post, rather than a guidepost? Why do we hang around so long in the past that it becomes hard to move on?

A: The concept of learned helplessness might provide some explanation to this question. When we focus on regrets from past actions, which cannot be changed, we feel helpless, since what is done, is done. Psychologist Martin Seligman used the term learned helplessness to explain this regretful past-oriented way of thinking. This concept originated in the 1960s when he did a research study with dogs that needed to jump over a barrier to escape mild shocks. He found that when the barrier was shut and they could not escape, they became apathetic and did not even try anymore, even after the barrier was lifted. He called that learned helplessness, as they learned from previous experiences that they were helpless–*even though they were not!*

Likewise, so many of our clients have the perception that their lives have spun out of control, leaving them with a sense of powerlessness. The psychological term, learned helplessness, explains that a common reason why people get depressed and give up is that they feel like no matter what they do, life spirals out of their control. Past abuse, unhappy childhoods, failed relationships, career detours and personal defeats lead them to the erroneous belief that they are victims with little control over their fate. They focus on the doors that are closed to them, instead of focusing on the open doors of opportunity at present.

*"When one door closes another door opens;
but we often look so long and so
regretfully upon the closed door, that we do not
see the ones which open for us."*

- Alexander Graham Bell

The Case of
Parental Regret

The Stinky Cheese says:

You blew it!
The problems your kids have are your fault!

The Swiss Wiz understands that regret is a type of phantom guilt. (The guilt that we should have known better, that we should have done better, and that we in some way should have been more powerful to make things different for ourselves and our loved ones.) Social Psychologist/Author Jane Adams writes in her book, *When Our Grown Kids Disappoint Us,* that guilt is a form of grief. This grief arises when parents watch their adult children fail to thrive. Despite the fact that parents are not as powerful in molding children as they might have thought, they still feel largely responsible for their children's shortcomings.

For example, if our gifted children turn out to be adults who cannot seem to get their life together, parents often rack their brains to figure out where they went wrong. Joshua Coleman, in *When Parents Hurt,* tries to lift the burden of blame off of parents. He reassures them that even parents who do most things right might have children with mental illness, substance abuse, job instability or relationship problems. He notes that some parents who try to do everything right are dismayed when their children show evidence of 'failure to launch.'

In his book, he reassures parents that just because you do your best to raise your children by providing a strong and nurturing household, you cannot be guaranteed they will turn out healthy and successful. Coleman offers solace to parents who are self-berating and scrutinize where they went wrong. His book is geared towards reassuring and soothing the parent who is plagued with guilt over their subtle parenting mistakes, real or imagined. It is this type of parental guilt that often becomes a major area of adult regret.

The Swiss Cheese Fairy of Life reminds us that giving up regret is not a once and done event. It is a process that takes time because this process does not travel in a straight line.

To reach acceptance, it is important to remind yourself that doing your best is all you can offer. By being patient and self-forgiving, you can accept not only yourself but others, too.

Remind yourself: When your kids were growing up, you were growing too!

**The Stinky Cheese laments what can't be changed.
His common refrain starts with:**

I wish I had….
Things shouldn't have...
I would be so much happier if...

and ends with:

Then things would have been better.
Then my life would have turned out.
Why me?

**The Swiss Wiz has long ago come to terms with the fact that what
is done, is done. He learns from the past instead of lamenting it:**

I learned that...and therefore...
I accept that it happened and…
I am thankful that...

and ends with:

I will figure out how to handle it NOW!
I will move through the disappointment.
I will give myself another chance.

*"All the king's horses and all the king's men
can't put the past together again..."*
- *Dale Carnegie*

Are You Like the
Little Engine that Should?

- I *should* be further along in my career by now.
- I *should* be smarter.
- I *should* be thinner.
- I *should* have a nicer house.
- I *should* have more friends.
- I *should* have known better.
- I *should* have taken that job.
- I *should* have done more with my life.

Suggestion: Label a jar with the word "Shoulds" and feature it prominently in your home. Remind yourself that this is where your shoulds belong–out of your head and into the jar! They are not doing any good trapped inside your head!

When you rid yourself of expectations of how life *should* be, then you become wiser and more accepting. When we surrender the shoulds we can take a huge step toward accepting things as they are.
This present-oriented focus allows us to feel more *whole!* With this healthy perspective, we develop a more here and now focus instead of a *woulda-coulda-shoulda* focus.

Woulda Coulda Shoulda

In their aptly named book, *Woulda, Coulda, Shoulda,* psychologist Art Freeman and writer Rose DeWolf depict the common human dilemma that plagues people all over the world; the tendency to revisit and rework choices and actions from the past. This penchant for regret over what seems so obvious in hindsight is an impediment to moving forward, and underlies anxiety, depression and self-sabotaging behavior.

"There is no shortage of mines to step on...Woulda coulda shoulda thinkers cannot describe the feeling without using past tense."
- Freeman and DeWolf

The authors offer encouragement to their readers that they can unlearn *woulda, coulda, shoulda* thinking by developing healthier thought habits. They encourage their readers to identify thinking that is extreme, blown out of proportion and perfectionistic. They caution against using all-or-nothing thinking that results in emotional disturbance and mental paralysis. They reason that by challenging irrational thought habits, people can get themselves to move from living in the past to living more fully in the present.

Freeman and DeWolf make the point that it is a common child-rearing practice to use time outs to make children think about what behaviors they did wrong. However, among adults, this practice can get out of hand and result in obsessive thoughts and rumination. Certainly, self-reflection and learning from one's mistakes can be healthy. But when taken to the extreme, obsessive self-reflection can be debilitating. They liken rumination to a cow chewing its cud–the cow chews the same material over and over again! It might work quite well for the cow, but not for people!

So instead of asking "Why" and "What if," how about moving on to "What now" and "What's next"?

You Cannot Turn Back the
Wheels of Time

- Forgive yourself for *falling short of your expectations.*

- Forgive yourself for *not knowing what you know now.*

- Forgive yourself for *poorly chosen words or actions.*

- Forgive yourself for *making decisions out of fear.*

Client Example:
A Lifetime of Atonement

I knew right away when I saw 64 year-old Kenny that he was a man who was among the walking wounded. The reason became clear to me the very first session: His frail wife, Edie, was wasting away from alcoholism, weighing less than 95 pounds, shunning the light of day and preferring to stay in their basement apartment and drink. They kept to themselves and were isolated from their community. Edie could barely walk, and self-medicated with whiskey and wine. If Kenny would refuse to go out and get more liquor, she reminded him of how he had betrayed her early in their marriage, and he would cave to her request out of guilt.

In therapy, he divulged that over 40 years ago he had a very brief affair. He has been haunted with regret over his actions ever since, in part due to almost daily reminders from Edie. She blamed Kenny for ruining her life and driving her to drink. It was only when Edie died at the age of 66 that he was released from the 40 years of penance, and he finally worked in counseling on forgiving himself and reconnecting with the outside world.

Sadly, it was her death which prompted him to begin his own healing.

What If Our Regrets Have a
Real Dollar Value?

- Are you still in disbelief that you held on during the tech bubble as you watched those high flyer stocks lose their value and evaporate to single digits?
- Are you kicking yourself for missing the big stock run-ups?
- Did you sell too low and buy too high?
- Are you berating yourself that your nest egg seemed to disappear in front of your own eyes?
- Are you down on yourself because of bad investments including buying your home at the peak of the housing bubble?
- Did your dreams of owning your own business end in rubble?

Ask the Therapist

Q: I lost so much of my wealth in the stock market and my house is a fraction of the value it used to be. Retirement is nowhere in sight. I should have known better! Now I will be working forever and will not be able to have the comfortable life I had been counting on. Why didn't I see it? How can I cope? How could I have been so foolish? How can I get over this?

A: Did you try your best with what you knew at the time? Did you do the best you could with the knowledge that you had? Use the lessons learned as an investment in your future, let them be a guide–not a persecutor. Let this experience put things in perspective–increase your focus on what is most important; relationships and your support system. A setback hardly means a catastrophe, unless we make it that way.

What Do We
Regret the Most?

In Neal Roese's book, *If Only: How to Turn Regret into Opportunity,* he offers four general areas where Americans commonly experience regret.

Regrets About Education*:* Roese cites not finishing school, not pursuing that advanced degree, or not applying oneself in school as common regrets. Since education is often a gateway to success, these regrets plague many Americans.

Regrets About Career Choices*:* Maybe you went blindly into a career, influenced by family and teachers, and realized later on that it wasn't a good fit. Perhaps your career did not give you the satisfaction you thought it would. Or maybe you were unable to find a suitable job and are now reminded of your family's disapproval of your chosen college major or not going to college at all! Or perhaps your career choice required too much time away from your family, and you cannot get that time back.

Regrets in Love*:* Whether it is a failed marriage, a relinquished relationship that is too late to rekindle, or discovering that the sourness of a relationship robbed you of your best years, regrets about love are high on the list for many people.

Regrets Over Parenting*:* Roese claims that among the people he interviewed, lack of parenting skills and impatience as a parent tops the list of major lifetime regrets. Other regrets on the list include having children too soon, waiting too long to have children, or not having them at all. Child-rearing differences between spouses, estrangement and distance from one's children were also sources of regret.

"Never look back unless you are planning to go that way."
- Henry David Thoreau

*"My mama always said you've got to
put the past behind you before you can move on."*
- Forrest Gump

From Remorse to Renewal– With the Help of

Counterfactuals!

In his research on regret, Roese studied counterfactuals. Counterfactuals are outcomes that could have occurred, but did not. It is not focusing on what did come true, but what could have!

Roese uses the example of tossing a coin–there are two potential outcomes, and only one comes true. If it lands with heads showing, then tails is the counterfactual, i.e. a possible outcome that did not come true. Yes, it had a 50/50 chance of occurring, BUT IT DIDN'T! Counterfactuals are everywhere–when you choose one of two ways to get to work, and end up getting stuck in a bad traffic jam and are therefore late for an important meeting, it is too late to change to the alternate route. Most people, of course, would be frustrated. But some take it to extremes and end up not only stuck in traffic, but also stuck in *should-have* thinking, berating themselves for choosing the wrong route. If you had known about the traffic jam in advance, you would have chosen the other route. However, the route you chose is an example of a counterfactual and there is no turning back! Kicking yourself over making the wrong choice will not help you get there any quicker! Such are the lessons of life! The next time you chose between the two routes, you might decide to listen to the traffic report or give yourself extra time in case the traffic jam was not a fluke. Thus, we can use our regrets to help us make better decisions in the future. As Roese asserts, "It is these roads not yet taken that provide us with an array of life lessons and choices that can strengthen us if we do not let it weaken us."

Do you subscribe to these counterfactual laments:

What might have been?

What if...?

Why couldn't it...?

Why couldn't I...?

In his book, *If Only: How to Turn Regret into Opportunity,* Neal Roese synthesizes years of research on regret, and offers his readers a new spin on the concept. Instead of looking at regret as something that is negative, he sees regret as potentially productive! YES! We can use regret to give us an impetus to solve problems and grow!

So regret can actually be really productive!

The Swiss Wiz advises:
Let's take Roese's advice and move on to productive regret!

An important lesson to learn in understanding regret is that we need a certain amount of regret to propel us to be better. Productive regrets can guide us and help us learn and improve.

Using the cheese analogy, many of us still love our Roquefort! Roquefort cheese is filled with mold, and it is this mold that provides the pungent flavor and distinctive bluish color. Sometimes mold is not so bad! Admittedly, Roquefort is a bit strong for many people and a life that resembles Roquefort will have more than its share of 'stinkiness.' Because of its pungent flavor, it is seldom eaten in the same volume as American or even Swiss–you can only take so much at one sitting! Its sharpness makes a strong impression and similarly the sharpness of life's regrets stay in our psyche and help to correct us for the future. It's a choice we make: Are we going to submit to the undertow of unproductive regret or are we going to spin a better and more successful tale from it, moving from unproductive to productive regret? After all, if we keep holding onto the past, how can we make room in our lives for the present?

> "If we fill our hours with regrets over the failures of yesterday, and with worries over the problems of tomorrow, we have no today in which to be thankful."
> - Unknown

Have a No Regret Policy...
Unless it is
Productive Regret!

**Don't second-guess
and regret
what you did
for love.**

*"I really can't regret any choice that brought
me one moment of love."*
- Martha Beck (Life Coach)

How to Turn
Unproductive
Regret...

It's all in your head!
Change your head and change your life!

Examples of Unproductive Regret:

- I can't get over losing her! I wish I didn't take her for granted!
- How could I have been so stupid? What was I thinking?
- I made such lousy choices!
- There have been so many ways it could have or should have worked out–the story of my life!
- If only I had left the job a long time ago.
- I messed up before, and I'm afraid of messing up again.
- I wasted the best years of my life!

...Into Productive Regret

**It just requires
a new perspective!**

Steps to Transform Your Regrets

- Life Coach Martha Beck writes of using regret as a springboard to take action.
- Even if you temporarily beat yourself up, get back to work!
- Going down memory lane is like looking at old photos, it's okay to take a trip down memory lane, just don't stay there! After you take the photo album out and peruse the pictures for a bit, put it away on the shelf.
- Use the corrective sharp sting of regret to make better choices now.
- How could it have been worse? In his book, *If Only*, Neal Roese calls this type of thinking, thinking downward. No matter how bad things got, it could have been worse!
- Write it out! Keep a journal so regret won't fester.
- As Nike® says, "Just Do It.®" Don't let fear stop you. A common regret is not taking action at all–often due to fear. Many regrets are for things not done, not just things that were done poorly.

*"There is nothing to regret - either for those
who go or for those who are left behind."*
- Eleanor Roosevelt

Client Example:
Little Margin for Error

Lisa was a 36 year-old veterinary technician that was plagued by low self-esteem. She dreamt of going to school to become a paralegal, but when asked why she had not realized this goal, she held her hand three feet off the table and claimed, *"I have this many regrets and failures and I can't afford one more!"*

Despite the large list she demonstrated with her hand, she actually could think of only two regrets–dropping out of college and losing her full scholarship. She could not think of any more grievous mistakes, but these regrets emotionally paralyzed her for the last 15 years. They defined her as a failure. It was as if she was walking on a tightrope with a very narrow margin, in fear of falling off again. She felt like she had to be flawless from then on.

In counseling, we worked on exploring her strengths instead of her perceived weaknesses. This helped free her from her unproductive, regretful thinking, which allowed her to pursue her dream to become a paralegal!

Don't you deserve a
Second Chance?

© 1996 Randy Glasbergen.

"Whenever something goes wrong,
I just push this little button and restart.
I wish my whole life was like that!"

Give up the Habit of Regret
Press the Restart Button NOW!

In the words of
The Swiss Wiz...

Holding on to unproductive regrets is like holding on to cheese way after its prime.

Regrets can be both productive or unproductive, it's all about how you view it!

Living with unproductive regrets is like being stuck in a hole.

Productive regrets can help you move on and gives you a fresh start!

In the words of
The Swiss Cheese Fairy of Life...

Choose today over yesterday.

Forgive yourself for not knowing everything when you were five!

Remind yourself you did the best you could at the time.

Be kind and gentle to yourself.

You are not alone! Move forward and fly with me!

Swiss Cheese
Tool Kit

Assembling the Metaphorical Tool Kit

In this first slice on regret, we will use a penny. As we demonstrated in this chapter, when you toss a coin and either heads or tails comes up, the side that did not come up is the counterfactual. Thus, counterfactuals are outcomes that could have occurred, but did not. With counterfactuals, the focus is on what might have been rather than what did, in fact, happen.

We will use the penny to help remind us that once a decision has been made, once an act has been done, once a consequence has occurred, there is no turning back. No matter how much you rethink what could have or should have happened, you have no control over changing it. No amount of rethinking and pondering will get the past to change. Being a Monday morning quarterback might offer great insight, but hindsight was not available at the time a decision was made. One of the nice things about this everyday item is that it reminds you of the importance of letting go of past regrets so you can live more fully in the NOW!

Second Slice

There is No Such Thing as a Perfect Slice of Cheese!

Transforming Mistakes and Failure Into Success!

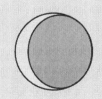

There is No Such Thing as a Perfect Slice of Cheese!

Transforming Mistakes and Failure Into Success!

Does fear of mistakes or fear of failure stop you from taking risks?

Do you put so much pressure on yourself to do things perfectly that you procrastinate and end up getting nothing accomplished?

Do you feel that your past mistakes stop you from moving forward?

Do you worry needlessly about what is already too late to change?

Do you let setbacks define you instead of regarding them as merely challenges to overcome?

Why is it that people treat others so much better than they treat themselves? Listen to your self-talk! Would you talk to anyone else like that? People are so free with harsh self-statements, such as "I blew it!" and "I'm a loser," but most would never think of saying such mean things to others!

Anything short of triumph, in our success-oriented society, is often viewed as a shortcoming and even failure. Whether it is getting a bad grade on a test or being let go from a job, do not let these perceived failures define you. Your self-worth remains intact! Join us in this chapter as we lead you through the maze of human imperfection and even failure, to ensure that your errors will be guides for the future rather than reasons to stay stuck in the past.

Any Way You Slice It...
...It Tastes Good!

Some people swear by cheese slicers, and others love good old fashioned knives. There is no right way to cut a piece of cheese. You can slice it, cube it, plain cut it, or grate it. Largely it is a matter of preference, and depends on whether you are cooking with it or eating it outright. Simply put, there is no such thing as a wrong way to break into the cheese.

Why is it so hard to apply this concept to the way we think?

Are you on a quest to be 'the best' and therefore hold unrealistic standards for yourself that leave little margin for error? Perhaps a lack of early validation from either family or a peer group leaves a gnawing hole in your self-esteem. Or perhaps you perceived early on that to make mistakes diminishes your own personal stock, despite reassurances to the contrary. By letting your shortcomings and fear of making mistakes define you, anxiety and a fear of failure can hold your self-confidence hostage. It is as if any mistake or setback becomes a reason to label yourself as a failure.

In our high school and college newsletters, we typically hear only about our classmates' successes and glory. We do not hear of the silent defeats and the crushing disappointments. How can you avoid falling into the trap of comparing yourself to those who have enviable and stellar accomplishments? How can you refrain from propelling yourself to mourn the loss of missed opportunities, leaving you to ask yourself, *"What in the world have I done with my life?"* Despite the outward success that some people have achieved, the sense that they are just a mere step away from "blowing it" makes them remain anxiously in a hyper state of alert.

Consider this–what if Christopher Columbus did not mistake America for Asia? Where would we be now?

"Failure is simply the opportunity to begin again,
this time more intelligently."
- Henry Ford

Letting Go of the
Fear

So let's say you strive to make no mistakes.
No holes, no goof-ups.
Does that make you perfect?
Or does that make you uptight and a bit rigid?
…or does that make you afraid to try?
Give up the fear of being YOU!

Therapist's Example: Looking Beyond the Fear

As a new therapist at my first job at the young age of 23, I felt very much out of my league in staff meetings. Everybody seemed so experienced and smart! What in the world could I add to a meeting? Week after week, my reticence at staff meetings was more noticeable. One day, my supervisor (rather drunk during a Christmas party) commented that I seemed more confident during my interview, and said he was annoyed at my timidity! I fooled nobody! I was crushed and realized that my fear of seeming stupid made me more ineffectual! I failed them! I failed myself!

I had nothing to lose–I had nowhere to go but up. *I had already failed!*

I sat myself down and wrote my irrational thoughts that limited me from feeling confident and speaking up on one side of a paper, and on the other side of the paper wrote a more rational response. It looked something like this:

46

Irrational Thinking	Rational Thinking
If I disagree, they might not like me.	I have to separate my ideas from ME!
I HATE making mistakes!	Hate is too extreme–I do not like it.
Everybody is so much smarter.	We are all unique–they are not better.
I wish I was more like them.	I will work on accepting who I am.
They probably find me annoying.	Even if they do, that does not make me inferior.
They probably think I am too young.	I can be competent despite my youth.

By looking at my list as a daily reminder, I used my inner conflict to work on changing some basic irrational beliefs that I carried around. This exercise prompted me to overcome my fears. I worked so hard at it that I eventually became a public speaker!

Failure as a
Precursor for Success

John Herman is proud to call himself a "business failure expert."
The speaker/author knows only too well about surviving after a huge failure.
His life has reflected the rise and fall, and rise again, of the American Dream.
In 1985, his publicly traded auto detailing company spanned 35 states and
the share price was 20 times more than the original price offering. John had it
made! With a private plane and three new cars, he was like a poster child for
the picture of self-made success in a capitalist economy.

This picture contrasted with a far bleaker portrait about a year later. His
company went under, causing him to trade the three new cars for a clunker.
John was broke, and was forced to move his family from an affluent suburb
to a low income rental, losing his boat and other byproducts of affluence.

He decided not to be one of those failed business owners who never try again.
He resolved to use what he had learned from his failed business venture to help
others in similar circumstances. He founded Equity Partners, a company in
which he claims has since worked with over 1,000 distressed companies. John
built on his stark failure to create a successful venture. Some companies he helps
salvage, while others he advises to dissolve. The lessons he learned from his own
failed ventures gave him wisdom to help others with their failures.

Below are some of his "Hermanisms" (axioms for business and life),
based on his book of the same title:

- It was only a failure if you failed to learn; otherwise, it was an
  experience.
- Failing builds character, even if nobody needs this much character.
- If you fall down, get back up.
- If only gold medals count, are all the other Olympians failures?
- Plan for success, not failure.

Success and Failure
One can actually lead to the other!

Copyright 2002 by Randy Glasbergen.
www.glasbergen.com

"My goal is to be a failure. If I reach my goal,
I'll feel successful and if I don't reach
my goal, I'll feel successful too!"

Success
Behind Most Every Success
is a Failure!

Successful Failures

Consider these famous people who made success out of mistakes and failures. If they stopped at their mistakes or failure, they would not have reached the prominence they did!

Oprah Winfrey was fired from a television reporting job and was told she was not cut out for TV.

Walt Disney's first cartoon production company, Laugh-O-Gram went bankrupt.

Abraham Lincoln failed in farming, business, his bids for Congress, Senate and the vice presidency. Before the days of bankruptcy, when his first general store went under, he lost everything including his horse and surveying equipment! Furthermore, he entered the Black Hawk War as a captain and came out as a private.

Dr. Seuss's first book, *And to Think That I Saw it on Mulberry Street,* was rejected by 27 publishing houses before being published.

Erin Brockovich had two failed marriages and was a single mom of three scraping by. She talked her way into a job as a secretary of a law firm where she investigated a pollution lawsuit. She ended up winning 333 million dollars for the working class residents affected by the pollution and was made famous in a movie starring Julia Roberts.

Michael Jordan was cut from his high school basketball team as a sophomore.

Bill Clinton lost his 2nd bid for re-election for governor in 1980 and went on to be one of the most popular presidents in history.

Winston Churchill failed the 6th grade.

Steven Spielberg failed to get into the prestigious film school at the University of Southern California, and instead studied English at California State University at Long Beach.

After one night at the Grand Ole Opry, Elvis Presley was fired after being told "you ain't going nowhere, son."

Steve Jobs was forced out from the company he founded at the age of 30, only to return years later to develop the iPod, iPhone, iPad and other innovations. At a well-known commencement address at Stanford University in 2005, he claimed this public failure was one of the best things that ever happened to him. As he said, "The heaviness of being successful was replaced by the lightness of being a beginner again, less sure about everything. It freed me to enter one of the most creative periods in my life."
He used this lesson as an example of how failure can open up new opportunities.

Did you know...

yellow sticky Post-it® Brand notes were actually a result of a failure?

In 1968, a team of 3M® researchers were perfecting adhesive tape when they came upon a sticky semi-adhesive. Since the adhesive was not strong, it was considered a failed project and researchers went on to develop a better adhesive. However, one of the 3M® researchers kept this failed experiment in mind. A few years later, he was frustrated at church when his bookmark kept falling out of his hymnal. Remembering the semi-sticky adhesive from a few years back, he went on to develop the indispensable and popular Post-it© Brand notes that were released in 1980 and are now used all around the world!

Even earlier in 1952, in another fortunate mistake for 3M®, a researcher created Scotchgard™ while working on synthetic rubber for airplane fuel lines. When a little of the rubber spilled on the research assistant's tennis shoe, they tried unsuccessfully to get it off. But as time went on, they noticed that while the shoe got dingy, the area with the spill remained clean. They knew they were on to something! A few years later, Scotchgard™ was out on shelves!

GLASBERGEN

Top Ten Steps
to Recover From a Mistake

- Admit that you made it.

- Forgive yourself.

- Don't turn things into catastrophes. Put it in perspective.

- Apologize; if apologies are in order.

- You can be wrong about something and still be okay.

- Remind yourself that being right is over-rated.

- Learn from it! Find the learning opportunity in the mistake.

- Stop ruminating over what can't be changed.

- Take action! Use the mistake to propel you into positive action.

- Let your mistake make you wise–do not get stuck in the "whys."

"Mistakes are part of the dues one pays for a full life."
- Sophia Loren

"Genius? Nothing! Sticking to it is the genius!
I've failed my way to success."
- Thomas Edison

Using Failures as
Stepping Stones

Who does not have their share of failures–those disappointments that interfere with dreams of happiness and the promise of self-worth? Who does not find situations in life that fall short of success, whether it is a failed marriage, not having the well-behaved children that you imagined you would have, or a job that falls far short of your expectations? The inevitable reality of your life missing the mark leads to one of two decisions: Resign yourself to a life of disappointment or shift gears and build on the disappointments. Shift from Plan A to Plan B to give yourself another chance for a fulfilling and rewarding life.

Harold Kushner, in his book, *Overcoming Life's Disappointments,* urges his readers to use the pieces of broken dreams, the shattered fragments of unrealized expectations as stepping stones to a new, more realistic dream. Using these fragments of unfulfilled hopes and dreams to learn life lessons can pave the way to wisdom and maturity. Perhaps you think things should not have turned out the way they did, but the reality is...*THEY DID!*

He urges his readers to proceed to build on their disappointments, to create more attainable dreams, and to become wiser from the knowledge they gained from their disappointments. As a result, life's disappointments and unfulfilled dreams offer opportunities for growth and healing to fashion new, more attainable dreams.

Edison had over 10,000 failed attempts before discovering the light bulb. As he said, *"I have not failed. I've just found 10,000 ways that won't work."*

"Many of life's failures are people who did not realize how close they were to success when they gave up."
- Thomas Edison

"Men succeed when they realize that their failures are the preparation for their victories."
- Ralph Waldo Emerson

Client Example:
Breaking Failure Into Stepping Stones

Karl was a 24-year-old college graduate who used his entire savings of $7,000 to hire software consultants and web designers to develop a web site for his internet start-up venture. He worked tirelessly developing his project. Despite the promise of this pursuit, it fell way short of his expectations and never got off the ground. Karl was crushed, feeling as if he had failed.

"I put my life on hold for so long, believing this would work. How could I have been so stupid? I was so foolish! I should not have been so idealistic—there were just so many flaws in the project! Why didn't I see this all along? I am such a jerk!"

In counseling, I mentioned Kushner's analogy of using disappointments and failures as stepping stones, rather than seeing them as millstones around his neck. I worked with him to break down how he could use his work for Plan B rather than Plan A. He was so bogged down with his failed decisions that he didn't take into account how some of those experiences were the stepping stones of later experiences. For example, the prototype of the website could be used as part of his portfolio when searching for a new job. The website was still proof of his creativity, even though the business did not succeed. Besides, he learned many lessons from this venture that could be applied to other work he may do in the future. It would only be a failure if he let it stop him from propelling forward. He could benefit from approaching future endeavors with the wisdom and lessons he gained from this failed project.

Using the stepping stones from his venture, he became a great job candidate. He was offered three jobs within a couple of weeks of one another-they were all high-level managerial jobs that required innovation and creativity. He used his website as proof to show future employers the type of project he could create, and realized that if he had not put effort into this endeavor, he might not have gotten his choice of jobs. Apparently, the potential bosses were not put off by his business failure!

"The difference between a stepping stone and a stumbling block is the way that you approach it."
- Saskia Shakin

Are You
Too Perfect?

People who are perfectionists can actually end up pushing other people away with their inflexibility and tendency to take themselves so seriously. All too often their constant need for perfection ends up sapping the energy out of them and those around them. The need to be right puts them on the defensive. DeWyze and Mallinger's book, *Too Perfect: When Being in Control Gets Out of Control,* reports that people who tend to be perfectionistic can be unpleasant to deal with, since the need to be right at any cost gets in the way of relationships. They write, "It's simply unpleasant to be around someone who always has to show he was right... And you can't teach anything to someone who can't acknowledge even tacitly that his understanding was ever deficient."

There's nothing perfect about being a perfectionist!

Highly imperfect in fact!

Yes, I agree. Quite flawed in fact!

Being so good can be not so good at all!

"Do not wait; the time will never be just right. Start where you stand, and work with whatever tools you may have at your command, and better tools will be found as you go along."

- *Napoleon Hill*

Perfectionism:
When Good is Not Good Enough

People who are highly confident are less likely to be perfectionists. Trying to do your best is different from perfectionism, because doing your best is within your control and perfectionism is unrealistic and out of your control. Perfectionism is like listening to an internal critic that is never satisfied. Perfectionism is often a mask for low self-esteem and anxiety.

In *When Perfect Isn't Good Enough: Strategies for Coping With Perfectionism,* authors Antony and Swinson focus on how feelings of not being good enough lead to problems such as extreme anger, social anxiety, depression, and issues with disordered eating and body image. They differentiate perfectionism from having high standards, which can actually improve your personal sense of effectiveness. They write that it all comes down to flexibility of beliefs–rigid expectations lead to a higher degree of perfectionism. One of their suggestions is to keep a Perfectionism Diary in which you write down thoughts and behaviors that are perfectionistic, to help with identifying situations and triggers for this type of thinking. They offer four steps for changing perfectionistic thoughts: Identify your thoughts of perfectionism, list alternative thoughts, consider the advantages and disadvantages to both ways of thinking, and then consciously choose helpful views after reviewing your various thoughts. They admit that although those four steps might seem easy to do, they actually take a lot of perseverance and practice.

Client Example:
Hey, This Was Supposed To Be Fun!

Carolyn is a 59-year-old woman who took
an art class for her personal enjoyment, but found
the class tedious due to her extreme perfectionism
and frustration over her lack of talent. She actually
got sick to her stomach and could not eat before each
class. "I always wanted to learn to paint, but I am so
frustrated with the way my work is coming out.
My instructor tells me I am too hard on myself,
but I can't help it!"

She learned to differentiate work from play, and gave herself the license to
not be so good at everything. Carolyn realized the importance of having fun
in her life, and how she made fun too much work! Especially in play, your
self-esteem need not be on the line. When she let go of the need to be the
model art student, she was able to transform her anxiety into excitement!

Ask the Therapist

Q: Is perfectionism really so bad? Shouldn't people try their hardest?

A: Mistakes are the inevitable cost of being human. Mistakes can be seen as learning opportunities. Fear of making mistakes could lead to shyness, obsessive thinking, anger, irritability, anxiety and depression.

Imagine you are walking on a tightrope and have very little margin for error–every misstep could lead to a devastating fall. Some people live their lives like that! Instead of giving themselves a wide plank to walk on, they walk on the tightrope of narrow perfectionist thinking. If they misstep once or twice, they have to catch themselves to avert a devastating fall.

Do yourself a favor–if you find yourself walking on a tightrope or even a thick rope, give yourself a wide plank with a lot more margin for error!

In his book, *How Good Do We Have to Be?*, Harold Kushner recalls when he was a child competing in a National Spelling Bee and was in the crying room after placing second. He bemoaned that in our society, anyone who is not first is often considered a failure. He correlates his feelings about placing second in the spelling bee to how people view life itself–anything short of perfection, making one serious mistake or misspelling, destroys hopes of success. As he wrote,

Life is not a trap set for us by God, so that He can condemn us for failing. Life is not a spelling bee, where no matter how many words you have gotten right, if you make one mistake you are disqualified. Life is more like a baseball game, where even the best team loses one-third of its games and even the worst team has its days of brilliance. Our goal is not to go all year without ever losing a game. Our goal is to win more games than we lose, and if we can do that consistently enough, then when the end comes, we will have won it all.

"Remember that fear always lurks behind perfectionism. Confronting your fears and allowing yourself the right to be human can, paradoxically, make you a far happier and more productive person."
- Dr. David M. Burns

In the words of

The Swiss Wiz...

- Failure might be necessary to achieve true success–don't be afraid of it!
- If you learn from them, there are no such things as failures and mistakes.
- Use the pieces of your failures and mistakes as stepping stones, not millstones.
- The only way to be perfect is to be the perfect YOU!

In the words of

The Swiss Cheese Fairy of Life...

- You need not prove yourself to be worthy–you are worthy no matter what.
- You are special without being perfect.
- Have fun trying and learning new things!
- I will be with you on the journey–relax and have faith in yourself as I do in you!

Swiss Cheese Tool Kit

Assembling the Metaphorical Tool Kit

This eraser helps remind us that mistakes are to be expected; that is what erasers are for! The eraser shows us that it is possible to recover from a mistake, and it's even possible to start over and try again.

Do you remember the saying, practice makes perfect? If you agree that mistakes are part of practice, how can you be perfect without them? IMPOSSIBLE!

If you use erasers in order to erase a mistake and start again, why don't you allow yourself the same in your life? Your self-worth does not need to be based on perfection! Let's say you use the eraser and erase something, and then make exactly the same mistake. What do you do? ERASE AGAIN!

Using an eraser is not a one-time offer. You can keep at it!

Sometimes it takes more than once or twice to mess up and learn your lesson. Some lessons are just harder to learn. As you feel more comfortable building on your mistakes, you will not make as many of them. You will be more accepting and less intent on noticing flaws.

Use your eraser to clear the way to new beginnings!

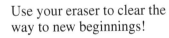

Mistakes offer the chance to transform your life!

The possibilities are perfectly ENDLESSSSS!

Third Slice

No Whine With the Cheese, Please!

Healthy Thinking for Life!

No Whine With the Cheese, Please!

Healthy Thinking for Life!

Think Straight, Feel Great!

Do rude people make you mad?

Does inclement weather give you the "blahs"?

Are there people in your life that can push your buttons?

Do you find that you compare yourself to others?

Do some people in your life annoy the heck out of you?

If the answers to any of these questions are "yes," then this chapter is for you! The correct response to all of the above items is actually "NO" because all these items are examples of impossible thinking! It is really your attitude and interpretation of events that stresses you out, not the external events or people themselves. As ancient philosopher Epictetus said 2,000 years ago, "Men are disturbed not by things, but by the view which they take of them."

Notice that all the above questions suggest that we are victims of external circumstances and that other people can control our feelings and perceptions. How untrue!

For example, does snow and cold upset you? Many people will answer "yes" to that question. But children, who love to play in the snow, or skiers who can't wait to ski on fresh powder, would answer "no"! Likewise, most people believe that traffic is a universal stressor. However, it is our perception of the traffic that causes us stress, not the actual detour or heavy car volume. Furthermore, consider if you were a traffic patrol officer. No traffic, no job (talk about stress!).

Are you a Stinky Cheese Thinker?

Just consider the following:

Please join me for a good whine! And why not have a stinky attitude?	**Please join me in stopping the *whine!* And why not have a healthier attitude?**
• *People are not raised with a moral compass anymore!*	• *Many people are raised with good values: It's not healthy to generalize.*
• *This country has just gone downhill!*	• *This country has also gone uphill in a lot of ways!*
• *This country is going backwards!*	• *Just think of advances in medical care, technology and science.*
• *It's not fair that life is unfair!*	• *Who in the world ever promised us a fair life?*
• *No one cares about anything anymore!*	• *A lot of people care quite a bit—and are truly passionate!*
• *People have no consideration!*	• *That is over-generalizing. No one is totally inconsiderate.*
• *He is always rude!*	• *At times, my feelings are hurt when he says things to me.*
• *He always hurts my feelings!*	

Client Example:
Breaking Free From Stinky Thinking

> *"I just never was a great people person. Other people seem to know what to say, but I have a hard time starting a conversation. I envy people who have the gift of gab. I'm afraid of embarrassing myself by saying something silly. That's the reason I hate cocktail parties. Even small talk at the office or in the company cafeteria can be very tough sometimes!" - Jerry*

Between both of us and our combined 60 years of counseling practice, we've heard Jerry's dilemma hundreds of times in various scenarios. His fear of embarrassing himself and saying the wrong thing is all too common.

I asked Jerry to pick a common situation to examine his way of thinking, and he picked going to his wife's family's social gatherings. He claimed he felt intimidated by his very successful brother-in-law, and overpowered by the entire family.

I explained to Jerry that feelings arise from automatic thoughts that we often cannot pinpoint. Together we tried to pin down some of the thinking which leads to anxiety. This is a sample of what he came up with:

George is smarter than me.

I am terrible at small talk.

I can't stand all the noise and people.

No wonder why he was so anxious! We examined the judgmental nature of all the statements and I taught him to challenge these interpretations with more rational ones. We replaced *terrible at* with the words *uncomfortable with,* and *I can't* with *I can, but don't like it.*

This is an alternate, more rational list that we devised together:

George is very intelligent, but his intelligence does not diminish my own.

It is unfortunate that small talk does not come easy to me.

I don't like to be around a lot of people and noise.

We discussed how his self-worth is not enhanced or diminished by comparisons with others and weighing his own personal value in comparison to the traits of others will ensure he never comes out ahead. Playing the comparison game will ensure a lifetime of dissatisfaction and envy. As Jerry learned to prevent extreme and irrational thoughts, his anxiety decreased and his enjoyment of family gatherings increased.

Do You Belong to the Stinky Cheese Club?

The Stinky Cheese says:

Please join me - Misery loves company! Let's share a good fine "whine" together!

I am just a realist! I see things more clearly than most people and do not sugarcoat things! Some people get all the breaks! I can't help but feel the way I do—you have no idea what idiots I have to put up with in my life! They cause me so much grief. Why should I forgive people who don't care if they drive me crazy?

The Swiss Wiz replies:

Try not to confuse realism with pessimism and out-of-control thinking. Rational, clear thinking is not sugar-coating. Rather, accept that your perceptions are not fact, but rather interpretations. As an adult, no one can upset you and cause you grief. You upset yourself over thoughts about what they are saying to you. The Stinky Cheese Club is not a club of which you would want to be a member!

The Swiss Cheese Fairy of Life consoles:

I can see that this type of stinky cheese thinking arises from a lot of pain and fear, and continues to cause a lot more pain. Anger masks sadness, and I want to help you heal. Please have as much faith in yourself as I have in you. I am that voice in you that tells you that you deserve better. There is so much beauty inside if you let it in! You don't have to feel alone.

"Pessimism is a waste of time."
- Norman Cousins

Quick Check:
Self-Inventory of Thought Habits

Consider an excerpt from this quick self-test we give out in our seminars to help people determine their thought habits.

Self-Inventory of Thought Habits

_____ 1. How many family members upset you?

_____ 2. How many times in a week do you think, "I can't take it anymore!"?

_____ 3. How many people do you know who are always critical?

_____ 4. How many things in your life are totally unbearable?

_____ 5. How many times in a month do you feel hopeless?

_____ 6. How many times in a month do you feel unworthy?

_____ 7. How many people push your buttons?

When we ask for a show of hands, we are constantly struck by how few people score in the 0-3 range. Totals range generally from 6 to about 12, with upwards of 20 and even more for many others. These distressing thought-habits explain the reasons so many people struggle with anxiety, life dissatisfaction and depression. The score for this test ideally is to be as low as possible because all of the items reveal irrational and extreme ways of thinking.

This self-test underscores the importance of recognizing irrational, exaggerated thinking. Short of dealing with catastrophic or life and death situations, none of these items are rational. They display black and white thinking which is blown out of proportion. Learn to be your own best friend–eradicate ways of thinking that only cause confusion and unhealthiness!

"There is nothing either good or bad,
but thinking makes it so."
- William Shakespeare

Garden Variety Types of
Counter-Productive Thinking

All-or-Nothing Thinking
Seeing things in black and white:
"He is evil" or "He is perfect."

Overgeneralization
Thinking in absolutes like always and never:
"You never have anything nice to say."

Fortune Telling
You think you can predict the future:
"Things will never change!"

Personalization
You take things too personally:
"They walked right by me–I did something wrong."

Playing the Comparison Game
You compare yourself to others, inviting low self-esteem:
"She's so much smarter and better than me."

Should Statements
Unrealistic expectations that leave one feeling inadequate:
"I should not still be in therapy after all this time."

Mental Filter
You pick out a negative event and dwell on it:
"I made a mistake and cannot get my mind off of it!"

Treating Interpretations Like Facts

People get mad, people get depressed, people get negative and people get anxious mostly because of one over-riding theme–they treat interpretations like facts. If only it was easier to see how our spin on things is at the root of most emotional problems! Unless you realize that you are thinking in ways that are not based in reality, you end up feeling like a victim, lost in a fog of misinterpretations. Most people do not know they can learn better thought habits. When you think in *stinky cheese* ways, you are actually lost in a cloud of confused thinking.

Learn to be a thought detective and identify distorted thinking–the type that digs you into a hole!

Below is a sample of how you can distinguish between the two major types of thought habits. Please note that we are not addressing themes related to abuse, tragedy and neglect. Rather, we are addressing everyday common issues that don't fall into the category of *HORRIBLE* or *TERRIBLE.*

Fictitious Thinking	Factual Thinking
Things always go wrong.	*Things do not often go the way I wish.*
Everything I do is wrong!	*I am not happy with things I've done.*
I shouldn't feel this way.	*I wish I did not feel this way.*
He makes me mad.	*I am mad at him.*
It's awful and terrible!	*It's unfortunate and disappointing.*
We always have this issue!	*Up until now we have had this issue.*
That makes me anxious.	*I am anxious about that.*
I can't change what I feel!	*I can change how I feel.*

An actual client's example of separating fact from fiction with the help of:

Fresh Start Thinking

The following is an example of a client's actual self-help assignment to combat mistaken thinking, reprinted with her permission. This is her actual attempt to replace self-harming thoughts with more healthy thoughts.

Fiction/Debilitating	Fact/Rehabilitating
It's too late.	Each day is an opportunity.
I've made too many mistakes.	I've made some choices that have not worked. All people do!
I blew it.	I've made some mistakes.
I have no future.	I have the wherewithal to create a positive, satisfying future.
I hate my life.	I can choose my moment-to-moment interpretations of my life.
It would be easier to give-up and not try.	Making changes and moving forward can be an adventure to enjoy.
I'm too old to start over.	Life is precious and worth enjoying.
I can't make it.	I have demonstrated to myself that I am capable, strong, and can make the best of life at any time I choose.

Making Mountains out of Molehills

"I thought I was falling into a vast, deep, dark pit of despair but it was only a pothole."

Ask the Therapist

Q: How can we deal with this boss who drives EVERYBODY crazy in the whole department? No wonder why his wife wanted a divorce! I can't help but be upset when he is around. He is loud and annoying, and there is nothing I can do about it since he is the boss! He makes me feel trapped!

A: Notice the all-or-nothing, extreme, blown out-of-proportion self-talk! No wonder you and your co-workers feel powerless and trapped. No one can make you feel anything–you are the gatekeeper of your feelings. Although you might be thinking you are making statements of facts, they are actually gross misinterpretations. You have allowed yourself to join the miserable ranks of the stinky cheese thinkers. Do you really want to be a part of that club? You can do better than that!

How can the boss drive people crazy? That is not possible. He is not driving them anywhere unless he gives them a lift in his car!

Notice the blown-out-of-proportion words you are using:

* Everybody * Crazy * Nothing * Trapped

Notice the blown-out-of-proportion ideas underlying:

I'll lose my job, if I stand up for myself.
He has the power to drive people crazy.
I'm trapped!

By being a good thought detective and identifying factual from fictitious thinking, emotions will be less immobilizing and more in control. In other words, you will have healthier, less toxic and less anxiety-riddled emotions. It's all in the way that you think!

The Power of a Thought

Yes, perception is the key!

Change your perceptions, change your life!

Are you a person who sees the glass half full or half empty?

They both look the same, but the way you view it means a world of difference.

Below is another visualization using a glass of water.

Activity: The Power of One Irrational Thought

Imagine having before you a clear glass of water.

If you put a drop of food coloring in a glass, you can see the water discolor. Thoughts are like that. Just one negative thought (like the drop of food coloring) can discolor your whole perspective. So don't let one nagging thought or concern discolor the big picture. Now imagine dropping many drops of food coloring, representing the many irrational, negative thoughts we often entertain during the day. You can imagine the muddiness that results when toxic thoughts are mixed together!

Let's summarize this chapter so far, so you won't drive yourself crazy with *STINKY THINKING!*

- Negative thinking leads to negative emotions.
- Replace irrational thinking with more rational thoughts.
- Clear thinking is the cornerstone for healthy behavior & emotions.
- Eliminate your distorted perceptions.
- In times of emotional turmoil, stick to the facts, not interpretations.
- Healthy thinking is solution-focused, not problem-focused.

Ask the Therapist

Q: You don't know my ex! If you did you would know why he makes me feel so furious! I can't help but lose my temper! How can I stop myself from losing my temper in front of our kids when he pulls all this crap? He leaves me to pick up the pieces! He drops them off without feeding or bathing them, making me do all the work, while he is "Good Time Dad"! How can I control my temper with him pulling that stuff?

A: Just because you feel out of control does not mean you need to be controlling over him! You are not going to change him. How about using this simple acronym to distinguish thoughts from interpretations:

W.A.I.T.
What Am I Thinking?

For example, if you stopped yourself and looked at your thoughts you would notice your thinking is causing your anger–you are telling yourself he is doing this to you, that he is making you mad, and that you can't handle it. You are making yourself mad because you keep on expecting that he should already be different rather than who he really is.

Stop and think about what you are saying to yourself. In the above example, you are blaming someone else for your emotional upset. You have a right to feel upset, but realize you are the only one that can control it and that you cannot control the other person. If he needs to change before you feel better, you might be waiting a long time. Watch out for anger that blames others for how you feel. *Anger is one letter short of danger!*

Sure, it's upsetting, but those upsetting thoughts don't need to consume you. Only you can change your thoughts. If you find that you are getting upset, remind yourself to stop, W.A.I.T. and reflect. If you have blown thoughts out-of-proportion, use your ability to separate fact from fiction–dispute toxic thoughts and replace them with more rational ones.

Or try the **Thought Stopping** method to help prevent ruminating: Picture a RED stop sign that alerts you to stop out-of-control thinking... and make sure you stop!

Wait, stop and take CONTROL!

In the words of

The Swiss Wiz...

- Remember: "Think Straight, Feel Great!"
- Remember to separate fact from fiction.
- Clear thinking limits the blame we put on others.
- Healthy thoughts help us let go of grudges and resentments.
- Be careful of thinking yourself into a hole!

In the words of

The Swiss Cheese Fairy of Life...

- With a clear head, we are more accepting and loving to ourselves and others.
- Critiquing is never the way to grow and thrive.
- Happier people glow from within!
- With an open heart, you will have an open mind.

Swiss Cheese
Tool Kit

Assembling the Metaphorical Tool Kit

We invite you to be a thought detective! This magnifying glass will help you examine your thoughts and feelings. The magnifying glass will remind you to look behind the interpretations to focus on the facts.

As we all know, magnifying glasses make things look larger. Do you realize that we do this with our thoughts? At times, we magnify issues and blow things way out of proportion. The popular saying "making mountains out of molehills" is exactly what many people tend to do when they catastrophize about things that are hardly life-threatening and are often forgotten in a short period of time. Distorted thoughts bring on immobilizing feelings and unhealthy behavior. Use this magnifying glass to zoom in on healthy ways of thinking.

Fourth Slice

If the Cheese is Ripe, DIG IN!

Be Proactive- Not Reactive!

If the Cheese is Ripe, DIG IN!

Be Proactive-Not Reactive!!

🧀 *Do you remember the NIKE® slogan, "Just Do It®"? Is this easier said than done?*

🧀 *Do you refrain from getting involved because you do not want to tie yourself down?.*

🧀 *Do you get too stressed out by the thought of trying new things?*

🧀 *Do you have too many loose ends and cannot seem to get organized?*

🧀 *Do you take charge or would you rather just charge things?*

As Mahatma Gandhi said, "Be the change you wish to see in the world."

The more proactive we are in our lives, the more we will feel empowered and in control. Do not wait for things to change and do not wait for people to change around you.

Making an action plan to get you moving will help you focus on what you can change instead of what you can't. Making each day count will fill your day with enthusiasm and hope. Getting involved in activities, organizations and groups offers a sense of community, leading to friendships and support. The saddest people are those who do not get involved, those who feel like a victim of circumstance and end up feeling alienated and lonely.

Take action and make a difference in your life!

Do you take control...
...or are life's events
...controlling you?

"Just once I'd like to seize the day before it seizes me!"

How much control do you have over your life?

Some people make things happen.

Some people watch things happen.

Some people wonder what happened!

Where do you belong? How about the people closest to you, in your family, at school or at work? Whether you are passive or active, you are making a choice. You might want to play it safe and not extend yourself too much. However, research has shown that when people feel a greater sense of commitment and pursue mastery over their lives, they will experience a higher degree of life satisfaction. The more you stay on the sidelines, the more likely you are to feel a sense of alienation and low self-confidence.

In other words...

> *"Things don't happen to us, we happen to things & we also are the ones that make things happen!"*
> - *Judy Belmont*

Give Yourself the Gift of Proactivity!

German Psychiatrist Victor Frankl (1905 - 1997) was the first to coin the term "proactive" in his 1946 hallmark book, *Man's Search for Meaning*. Through his experience during World War II in a Nazi concentration camp, where he lost his wife, parents and other family members, he used this term to describe someone who would take charge of his attitude and feel in control rather than feel at the mercy of circumstances. He tenaciously held onto the idea that no matter how bleak the situation, one need not be a victim in reaction to circumstances, but that everyone has the ability to take control of one's attitude.

Almost a half century later, Steven Covey, in his highly-acclaimed book, *7 Habits of Highly Effective People*, used the term "proactive" as the first essential habit of people who are successful.

Covey, like Frankl, also focused on the importance of having a sense of control over one's attitude. He also differentiated those who were *reactive* vs. *proactive*.

Covey underscored the importance of taking charge rather than waiting for things to happen; to plan and organize using a sense of personal mission. It takes conscious effort and planning to make changes in your life, rather than just react to circumstances. By being proactive instead of reactive, less time is spent fighting fires when something unplanned occurs and you will be more likely to be self-directed in achieving personal goals. This sense of personal responsibility can be viewed as *victor* mentality vs. *victim* mentality. A *victor* will not blame others for his/her misfortune and will not indulge in *victim* self-talk.

Client Example:
Her Lips Felt Sealed Shut

In our marital counseling session, Donna visibly quivered as she admitted the reason why she froze in our couples' sessions. Although she was very talkative in our individual sessions, she feared her husband would be upset about something that she said in our couples' session and she would be punished by his coldness for days afterward. Out of fear of disappointing him and saying something that could upset him, she admitted, "I feel like my lips are sealed shut." She found through counseling the courage to become more proactive by saying what she felt, and stopped taking responsibility and feeling guilty about his reactions. This attitude helped her quell the fears that previously prevented her from being proactive instead of reactive. Their relationship improved when she no longer was afraid to speak her mind.

Don't expect it to be easy!

One thing that stops people from diving in to a difficult task is that it seems formidable or too hard. Maybe they don't know that sometimes the most difficult things are the most rewarding and help us the most. If you don't expect things to go easy, the daunting aspect of an act will not intimidate you. Hard work can be rewarding, and yes, even fun. Easy tasks that are repetitive and simple can be boring. The old adage, "Hard work pays off" could not be closer to the truth!

The more you put yourself into something, the more you will get out of it!

"Ask not what your country can do for you, but what you can do for your country."
- John F. Kennedy

"The world is not dangerous because of those who do harm, but because of those who look at it without doing anything."

- Albert Einstein

Why Wait?
Sometimes you just need to jump in!

Are you the type to take a lot of time putting your toe in at the pool or ocean, gradually getting in the water, or do you just jump in? Neither is the wrong way, although some tasks might be more easily approached by the "Just Do It®" method.

> I oversaw a move recently for a friend who needed to be out of town on moving day. After three men worked for four hours until 7 PM to load up the truck, one mover lamented that he wouldn't get home until after midnight since they needed to bring everything to their storage facility to unload. When I asked why they didn't wait until tomorrow to unload the truck he explained that they already had a full day scheduled for another job. So I asked how he could manage so much laborious work, and he answered with a question, "What does Nike® say?" I looked at him blankly not understanding what he meant. He replied, "JUST DO IT.®"
>
> It worked for Nike®–why not for you?
>
> In 1988, Dan Wieden, a marketing executive for Nike®, liked the company's can-do attitude and said in a meeting, "You guys just do it," which inspired their iconic slogan. They went on to surpass Reebok®, their main competitor at the time, and make history with the growth of their company, spurred by a very strong slogan.
>
> The appeal of the slogan, its simplicity, as well as the self-empowerment of the little phrase, can help you if you let it.

Just Do It.® Get out of your own way!
It's that simple!

Have a Can Do Attitude!

Help to untie the can "(k)nots" into "cans."

We often suggest that clients put a can on their desk reminding them of the importance of the "can" attitude. Some clients choose to cover it with paper and write out some can-do messages that reflect a can-do mindset.

- If you had a can featured prominently on your desk, what would it say?
- The more you think in terms of can "(k)nots" the more you will feel tied up into knots!
- How tight are your knots, how inflexible are your can "(k)nots"?
- Loosening the grip of the knots will keep you in a can-do mindset!

"You gain strength, courage, and confidence by every experience in which you really stop to look fear in the face. You must do the thing which you think you cannot do."

- Eleanor Roosevelt

What is your Proactivity Quotient?

The following checklists help you determine how proactive you are in terms of your attitude and in your actual behavior. Add the two scores together and find out your Proactivity Quotient.

In terms of life satisfaction, your P.Q. is more important than your I.Q.!

As folk singer, Joan Baez once said, "Action is the antidote to despair."

Proactive Mindset Quotient - Tapping into the power within

Next to each item put the number that best applies.

Strongly Disagree				Agree			Strongly Agree		
1	2	3	4	5	6	7	8	9	10

1. _____Much of what happens to me is merely a matter of my own doing, not luck.

2. _____Stress exhilarates me just as often as it works against me.

3. _____I refuse to allow regrets and disappointments cloud today.

4. _____I tend to think rationally and optimistically.

5. _____I focus on what I can change rather than focus on things I can't.

6. _____I tend to focus on my successes rather than my short comings.

7. _____I do not hold onto grudges and tend to forgive others.

8. _____I am more concerned about how I view myself rather than be preoccupied with pleasing others.

9. _____Although I certainly would prefer that people like me, I do not excessively seek or need approval.

10. _____I feel I have a great deal of control over what happens to me.

11. _____I have a healthy sense of humor; laughing at life's imperfections.

12. _____I feel gratitude in life rather than focus on what's lacking.

13. _____I am more present-focused than regretful.

14. _____I am filled more with pride than self-blame.

15. _____I have confidence that I do things competently and take pride in my achievements.

Total Score _____

Inner Empowerment Quotient: Total score ÷ 15 = _____

Proactivity in Action Quotient

Next to each item put the number that best applies.

Strongly Disagree				Agree			Strongly Agree		
1	2	3	4	5	6	7	8	9	10

1. _____I tend to be organized and do not procrastinate.

2. _____I have a close network of friends and family.

3. _____I have at least one person in my life to whom I can self-disclose.

4. _____I enjoy making connections and meeting new people.

5. _____I am not embarrassed to promote myself.

6. _____I communicate assertively, confidently, and with tact.

7. _____I am good at breaking down goals into manageable steps.

8. _____I feel a strong sense of network and community.

9. _____I take care of myself in terms of nutrition and exercise.

10. _____I would describe myself more as a leader than a follower.

11. _____I love to help others.

12. _____I allow others to help me.

13. _____I do not rely on non-prescription drugs or alcohol to help me cope.

14. _____I am financially responsible and have not accrued a lot of debt.

15. _____I have a sense of commitment and passion in some areas of my life.

Total Score _____

Proactivity in Action Quotient: Total score ÷ 15 = _____

Proactivity Quotient

Add both totals: _____

Proactive Mindset Quotient: _____

+

Proactivity in Action Quotient: _____

Divide the total by two to get your Proactivity Quotient:
_____

Where do you fit on their scale?

Low Power	Average Sense of Power	High Power

1	2	3	4	5	6	7	8	9	10

- Notice if there are areas in which you would like to score higher.
- Figure out an action plan.
- What can you do about it?
- Write it down.
- Make steps to change–concrete steps.
- Give yourself rewards and reinforcements if you take action.

How did you do? How can you use this information?

How about trying something new each day to work on boosting your P.Q.?

Ask the Therapist

Q: I keep on putting things off further and further, before you know it I have so much to do that I do not know where to start. I just can't seem to get myself going. HELP!

A: How about trying the Swiss cheese method of dealing with procrastination?

In his book, *How to Get Control of Your Time and Your Life,* Alan Lakein encourages people to use a Swiss cheese approach. Take little bites at a time! Tackle something you want to do by breaking it into small bites like the holes in the Swiss. If you plan your time and take 5-minute intervals to get a project done, once you get over the hump (or out of the hole) you are more likely to stick with it! Chip away at large tasks by taking bites, or making small holes. He encourages his readers to create a list and carry it around–when you have extra time, like when you are waiting for an appointment, you can refer to the list and take a bite.

He writes, "The underlying assumption of the Swiss cheese approach is that it is indeed possible to get something started in five minutes or less. And once you've started, you've given yourself the opportunity to keep going…Swiss cheese is supposed to lead to involvement." Eventually you will make so many holes in your task that it will be accomplished!

As you can see, we are not the only authors that liken life to Swiss cheese!

Perfection and Procrastination

It has been commonly thought that the greatest procrastinators were actually perfectionists who were so fearful of making mistakes that they end up doing nothing at all. Fear appears to be at the foundation of perfectionism—the fear of not doing things right can cause feelings of paralysis and inaction.

The Stinky Cheese says:

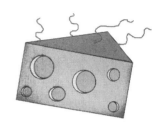

I have so much on my plate, there is no way I can get all this done! It's useless!

The Swiss Wiz replies:

I do not pay much attention to generalities, especially when they are out of my control.

You know how to approach this overwhelming list?

DO ONE THING AT A TIME!

You have only three things to do?
Do one thing at a time!
You have 101 things on your plate?
Do one thing at a time!
You have 148 items on your to-do list?
The same principle applies:
Do one thing at a time!

The Swiss Cheese Fairy of Life adds:

Just trust yourself; instead of worrying about not doing it right, just try your best. That is certainly good enough!

Perfectionists have harsh judgments of themselves, yet are so sensitive to the slightest hint of criticism from others! How is that for a paradox?!

More Tips on Getting Organized

In *The 25 Best Time Management Tools and Techniques,* Dodd and Sundheim recommend many tips and tools to get organized. Below are just a few:

1. Write it down, or dictate.

Get your ideas and plans out of your head and onto paper or into a recorder. Whatever you do, don't keep them trapped in your head!

2. Make sure you clarify your goals.

If you don't clarify what the purpose is, you might not be as motivated to get working on a task. By clarifying your goals and your values, you will remind yourself why you want to take action in the first place. It can help you stay on track.

3. Be SMART! Make sure your goals are:

Specific: Be specific about your ultimate goal.
Example: *"I want to be more fit."*

Measurable: An effective goal is one that can be objectively measured.
Example: *"I want to lose ten pounds."*

Achievable: Make sure your goal is realistic to achieve.
Example: *"I will try to lose 1 pound every other week."*

Realistic: Be realistic when you set goals.
Example: *"Since I am traveling, it is not realistic to work out four times this week."*

Time bound: Set a target deadline to work towards.
Example: *"June 21st, five months from now, is my target date to lose 10 pounds."*

4. Keep your space clean and organized.

A cluttered space reflects a cluttered mind. When you keep your desk, closets, shelves, etc. organized you will likely experience a lot less stress. Clutter can be very time consuming to wade through. If you have a place for everything, you will spend less time looking for things. You will have less need for upkeep. It is easier to have a clear mind when your papers are not buried high on your desk. If you feel scattered, does your house or office reflect your state of mind?

A Place for Everything

Most organizational specialists agree that it is important to have a place for everything. Looking for things, such as your keys or glasses, is a time waster and causes excessive anxiety, especially if you are in a hurry. The more you organize your surroundings, the more you will feel a sense of control. In *One Year to an Organized Life*, Regina Leeds gives a month by month approach to streamlining your life, from organizing your home, systematically getting rid of clutter, to getting your finances organized. She gives tips on how to get rid of miscellaneous paper piles and make the dining room table a place to eat once again!

Julie Morgenstern, in *Time Management from the Inside Out* recommends a three-pronged strategy to manage your time:

STEP 1: *Analyze:* Analyze what needs to be done.

STEP 2: *Strategize:* Develop a strategy of how you will approach it.

STEP 3: *Attack:* Get into it and do it!

Morgenstern emphasizes that when it comes to organizing, all too often, the first two steps are neglected which makes the attack step less efficient. Analyzing and strategizing will allow you time to observe your patterns so that you can pinpoint what does and does not work for you—this ensures that your action plan will be realistic and attainable.

Client Example:
Getting Rid of Clutter

Harry was a 57-year-old insurance agent who was referred by his doctor for therapy due to extreme anxiety, stress and difficulty sleeping. When asked what keeps him awake at night, he responded that he felt like he could not get a handle on his life. He claimed he had too many loose ends and that his inbox was continually overflowing.

Upon further questioning, it became apparent that Harry's file cabinets in his home office were full of papers back to the start of his business 30 years ago. With no room in his cabinets, he started making piles on his desk and the floor. It was a daunting task to go through drawers bursting at the seams, as well as the cluttered desk and floor. We devised a plan in which every day he would tackle sorting through his files for a half hour, discarding old policies and unnecessary papers. He stuck to our plan until he created a saner workspace. His clean work area reflected a new calm and his anxiety decreased.

The Large Chunk Fallacy

People who are not familiar with *The Swiss Cheese Method* of dealing with procrastination, in which small bites are taken frequently to tackle a project, might end up procrastinating. They wait for the right time to tackle a task that seems overwhelming. This mistaken notion that you need large chunks of time to get anything done will lead to delays and a sense of powerlessness. The notion of "hurry up, get it all done" might actually slow you down! When the task seems overwhelming you might spend your time avoiding things rather than tackling them. This is often a result of perfectionist thinking. The task itself feels so big that you think you need big blocks of time, and then can never seem to find the time or motivation. This *Large Chunk Fallacy* often leads people to wait until the last minute, and they find themselves putting things off because they think they have no time or energy to really do it right.

Do not disregard the importance of taking small methodical steps to getting a job done. Do you subscribe to the notion that unless you do it all your efforts aren't really worth anything? This all-or-nothing thinking gets many of us stuck. Try focusing on going in the right direction rather than *needing to get it all done!* You'll end up accomplishing a lot more by taking small steps and will be more likely to enjoy the process along the way!

The Stinky Cheese complains:

I'm not going to do anything until it is right.

The Swiss Wiz offers solutions:

I will be more process-oriented than product-oriented.

I will focus on starting, not when I need to finish.

Are you a "Doer" or a "Stew-er"?

Whatever the reasons for procrastination, it not only robs you of time and the rewards of decisive action, but it leads to feelings of anxiety and undue stress. People who procrastinate have more difficulty feeling satisfied with themselves and their lives. A general rule of thumb: The more you tend to procrastinate, the more you will feel chronically unfulfilled and dissatisfied.

Is your self-talk positive or do you hold yourself back with a lot of immobilizing words?

The Stinky Cheese Uses Procrastination Talk:

I should	It's so hard	I have to
I hate to	If only I	I can't

The Swiss Wiz Uses Proactive Talk:

I would like to	I want to	I will
I am going to	I am	I can

Take the Swiss Wiz Challenge–

Don't Stew—DO!

Analyze your patterns and identify strategies that work for you:

- Have a vision–create a personal mission.
- Plan ahead, develop an action plan.
- Follow the action plan–leave procrastination to the procrastinators!
- Create your own opportunities.
- Anticipate future outcomes as well as obstacles.
- Plan! Don't let yourself be thrown off-guard.
- Don't hesitate, don't wait—and don't be late!

Client Example:
Make a List!

Jeannie and her husband, Mike, saved up money to renovate their kitchen, replacing outdated, but still usable appliances. They both agreed that Jeannie would scout out the new appliances and decide on what she liked before showing it to Mike. However, two years had passed and Jeannie had not even started. She was overwhelmed with choices and was afraid of making decisions.

In fear of making a wrong choice, Jeannie did not act at all. I encouraged Jeannie to make a list of what needed to be done to renovate her kitchen. On that list, she broke the task down into all of the steps she needed to do, and then she prioritized the items. By breaking this seemingly overwhelming task into smaller, more manageable steps, she already felt relieved.

Since she was perplexed as to the best place to get her appliances, I reassured her that walking into a store does not require a commitment to purchase anything. Being comforted with the notion that looking did not necessitate a commitment, she started shopping around. After a few weeks, it became clear to her what she liked, and in narrowing she became less fearful about making decisions.

One thing that helped Jeannie was the realization that the decision was important, but not life altering. Sure, she was spending a lot of money and wanted to do it right, but there were many ways of re-doing her kitchen that would be pleasing to her and her family. With this mindset, she allowed her sense of humor to lighten the heaviness of her decisions, and this did wonders in lightening up her attitude. Her choices did not have dire consequences, and as she relaxed her attitude she had more fun in the process. Jeannie and her family ended up delighted with her newly remodeled kitchen.

In the words of
The Swiss Wiz...

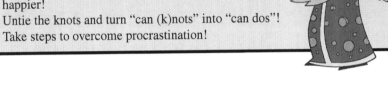

- You can make things happen!
- Try to move from passivity to activity–you will be happier!
- Untie the knots and turn "can (k)nots" into "can dos"!
- Take steps to overcome procrastination!

In the words of
The Swiss Cheese Fairy of Life...

- Do not let fear stop you from trying!
- Believe you can do it and you will find more strength in yourself!
- By taking chances, you are showing courage!
- Believe in yourself–as I believe in you!

Swiss Cheese
Tool Kit

Assembling the Metaphorical Tool Kit

This toy soldier represents proactivity. It reminds you to take control, and arm yourself against apathy, passivity and procrastination! Being proactive takes a lot of courage. The soldier will remind you to "soldier on" even when you are tired, afraid, lonely or unsure of yourself. Remind yourself that by refusing to give up or put things off, by soldiering on, you will reap more benefits in life than watching from the sidelines.

Be brave, be strong, meet challenges with confidence and have faith in yourself!

Fifth Slice

Living Whole Despite the Holes!

Mindfulness and Spirituality

Living Whole Despite the Holes!

Mindfulness and Spirituality

Do you find yourself driving in your car from one place to another, not realizing how you got there?

Are you spending too much time thinking about what already happened–or what is going to happen–so that you are not aware of what really is happening?

Do you spend a lot of time in life's waiting room, waiting for preconditions of happiness to pan out?

Do you think that something from the outside will be the key to your inner sense of happiness?

Are you so focused on getting things done that you do not enjoy the experience along the way?

If you are like most people, you might find yourself looking outward for the type of life satisfaction that can really only be found from within. Some have turned to alcohol, drugs, unhealthy relationships, workaholism, or even sexual addictions to quell the emptiness within. When life throws a curve ball, and things do not turn out as hoped, contentment and fulfillment might seem a bit out-of-reach. Others look for the latest electronics, clothing, cars and various material possessions that entice them, offering the promise of fulfillment and a rush of happiness. Yet, looking for fulfillment through stuff will let you down after the temporary high of obtaining it. Fulfillment comes from within, not from things around us.

These preconditions to happiness never fail to disappoint and at times seem to break our hearts. This is where spirituality and mindfulness offer hope for the seeker who often finds himself saying, "When I [fill in the blank], then I'll truly be happy!"

In an interview on NPR based on a documentary about his life, singer-songwriter Bill Withers (*Ain't No Sunshine, Lean on Me, Just the Two of Us*) offers the wisdom he shared with his children to emphasize the importance of accepting reality as it is.

"... it's OK to head out for wonderful, but on your way to wonderful, you're gonna have to pass through all right. When you get to all right, take a good look around and get used to it, because that may be as far as you're gonna go."

– *Bill Withers*

Are You Really "Here"?

Let's try a little exercise. Look around the room you are in and look closely at everything that is *BLUE*. Take a close look now. Got it?

Are you aware of what is going on around you now? Being mindful means that you are present, focused and aware of what is around you.

Now, close your eyes and tell me everything that you saw in the room that was *YELLOW!*

If you are like most people, chances are you were so focused on looking for things that were blue that you mostly ignored the yellow.

We live our lives like that. We often are looking at certain things in certain ways and fail to really see what is all around us!

What is it called when you are present in the moment?

Mindfulness

YES! Being in the present...AT PRESENT!

It's about not waiting for life to change to be truly happy. It's about RIGHT NOW!

> *"The secret to life is not in having more,*
> *but in wanting less."*
> *- Ancient Chinese proverb*

Do You Have a in Your Sense of "Wholeness"?

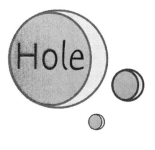

When we used the analogy of being in a hole, it refers to feeling stuck. However, if we really are in the zone of acceptance and spiritual wholeness we can free ourselves by being present-centered. To be present, one needs to stop the incessant chatter of a "monkey mind"–a mind that races at 200 miles per hour. In place of these racing thoughts, you can calm your monkey mind with a focus on the present–accepting what is rather than what was or what should be.

Yes, we can be at peace and feel whole no matter how deep we are in the hole.

These are the signs of being in the now:

- We feel fulfilled with life as it is at present, not what it is supposed to be.
- We're not waiting for a better day.
- We're not waiting for a bad mood to blow over.
- We're not waiting for our lives to change.

So paradoxically, the more you make peace with the hole, the less you will be in the hole!

Once we open our hearts and minds to the present, we actually become whole.

In Other Words,
BE HERE NOW!

In 1971, Harvard Professor of Psychology, Richard Alpert, a.k.a. Baba Ram Dass, wrote the spiritual classic based on Eastern spirituality, *Be Here Now*. After living a life of anxiety and discontent, he left his Harvard job and turned to drug experimentation (in particular LSD) with his well-known buddies Dr. Timothy Leary and Aldous Huxley. Not finding the answers he was looking for, he turned to Eastern spirituality and traveled to India on a spiritual quest where he found his spiritual teacher and Guru, Maharaj-ji. His guru gave him the name Ram Dass which means "servant of god."

Hindu spiritual meditation became his adopted practice, and he imparted the teachings he learned in his playfully written and illustrated book, *BE HERE NOW!* In his groundbreaking work, he addressed the spiritual emptiness of materialistic society, and urged his readers to look within rather than outside of themselves in their quest for spiritual fulfillment and peace.

> *If we're not in the HERE & NOW*
> *No matter how much food*
> *We put in our bellies*
> *It's never going to be enough*
> *And that's the feeling of Western man*
> *It's not enough*
> *He's got it all going in*
> *As fast as he can shovel it*
> *He's got every sensual gratification*
> *He can possibly desire &*
> *It's not enough*
> *Because there's no*
> *HERE & NOW-ness about it*
> *- Baba Ram Dass in Be Here Now*

During the late 60's and early 70's, Eastern spirituality became fashionable for those who were seeking enlightenment. Famous superstars like the Beatles turned to Eastern spiritual practice after finding that success, fame and materialism did not provide the sense of peace they were looking for. Eastern spiritualism, with its focus on mindfulness and radical acceptance has become more widely a part of mainstream American culture, laying the platform for the popularity of meditation and yoga practices.

To attain a more mindful way of living, try a yoga class, try meditation, or just make an effort to focus less on yesterday and tomorrow in order to open yourself up to what is happening today!

So get yourself out of the hole by opening yourself to the here and now!

Taking Time to be Mindful
Client Example:
Finding Something That Was Missing

Judy

Carrie is a thirty-nine year old college-educated woman who left a successful career in advertising to raise her three children. Although Carrie made the choice to be a stay-at-home mom, she still felt that she shortchanged herself when she left a profitable and creative career. Upon close self-examination, Carrie realized that she had given up a big piece of herself by putting her creative passions on hold. In college, she was an art major who loved abstract sculpture. Since having her children almost nine years ago, Carrie had given up her creative and artistic pursuits both personally and professionally, focusing on more mundane matters. She realized that this was a big piece of her angst, and began to devote time to her art. When she was working on her sculpture she found herself totally engaged in the process. As if, time ceased to exist. Taking time for artistic passion offered her a sense of peace and fulfillment which made her more satisfied in her role as wife and mother.

What type of things can you think of that you have not done, either because you tell yourself you don't have enough time, or because you don't make time for things that you might regard as frivolous or unimportant?

*"You cannot travel the path until
you have become the path itself."*
- Buddha

*"Do not dwell in the past, do not dream of the future, concentrate
the mind on the present moment."*
- Buddha

The Way of the Tao

Popular self-help author, Wayne Dyer, has written many books combining the principles of psychology with spirituality. Dyer offers his audience a bridge between Western and Eastern thought, epitomized in his book on the wisdom of the *Tao Te Ching*. In *Change Your Thoughts, Change Your Life: Living the Wisdom of the Tao,* he combines the Western principles of cognitive psychology with the soul-searching spirituality of Eastern thought. Dyer spent a year pouring over hundreds of translations for the 81 sayings of the *Tao Te Ching (The Great Way),* using the ancient scriptures to address the spiritual needs of modern man. Dyer responds to man's fundamental need for meaning in today's fast-paced world by exploring the wisdom of the ancient scriptures were written 25 centuries ago. He writes that the teachings are just as relevant today.

Tao Teaching:

"Remind yourself daily that there is no way to happiness;
Rather, happiness *is* the way."

Dyer writes, "You may have a long list of goals that you believe will provide you with contentment when they are achieved. Yet, if you examine your state of happiness in this moment you'll notice that the fulfillment of some earlier ambitions didn't create an enduring sense of joy. Desires can produce anxiety, stress and competitiveness, and you need to recognize those that do. Bring happiness to every encounter in life."

Tao Teaching:

"Stop the chase to be a witness."

Dyer writes, "The more you pursue desires, the more they will elude you...stay appreciative of all that you receive."

Mindfulness and Change...
It's All in the Dialectics!

Marsha Linehan, from the University of Washington, spearheaded a new movement in the field of psychotherapy for the most challenging and hard-to-treat clients. She called her practical, life skills approach to treatment *Dialectic Behavior Therapy* (DBT). The word, *dialectic,* means *opposite,* and Linehan used this term to point to the fact that life is full of conflicting and opposing wants and needs. For instance, if I eat a big dessert I am undermining my desire to lose 10 pounds. I have two conflicting (or dialectical) needs; I want to feel better about my body, but at the same time want the immediate gratification of eating a slice of yummy chocolate cake. In DBT, the need for change is combined with the need for non-judgmental acceptance of things as they are. Although these two concepts seem to be contradictory, both change and acceptance are important ingredients for a healthy life adjustment.

Linehan teaches that when you are mindful, you can tolerate a higher level of distress as you learn ways to distract, self-soothe, and accept rather than resist what you cannot change. As an example of mindfulness, Marsha Linehan differentiates between mindfully describing and describing in a judgmental way. She offers this simple demonstration: Linehan makes a grimacing face and asks her audience to *mindfully describe* what they see. Although many people use terms such as anger, upset, and confusion, she makes the point that to be truly non-judgmental and observant, they would cease to make interpretations at all. To mindfully describe requires sticking to the facts–describing that her lips are pursed, eyebrows furrowed, while refraining from using judgmental terms that infer anger or confusion. By practicing this habit of *mindfully describing,* focusing on observing rather than interpreting, you bring your awareness to the forefront of your life.

What They Say About Mindfulness

The Swiss Wiz

- The mindset of *mindfulness* helps us be at peace with the way things are.
- It allows us to see things in a very different perspective.
- We are more satisfied when we are present and accepting.
- We are more likely to appreciate harmony and peace of mind.
- Mindfulness helps us see order through chaos.

The Stinky Cheese

- Is too busy to stop to be mindful.
- Thinks mindfulness is overrated.
- Doesn't like nature to begin with–there are too many bugs!
- Prefers being a human "doing" than a human being.

Mindfulness With a Raisin

Did you miss your lunch today? The question isn't asking if you skipped lunch, but rather did you munch without true awareness of what you were eating? Was the lunch finished before you registered that you ate too fast and hardly noticed what you were eating? In their book *The Mindful Way Through Depression,* Williams, Teasdale, Segal and Kabat-Zinn offer this exercise that can unleash the healing power of mindfulness.

"Take one raisin and spend minutes holding it, looking at it, touching it, smelling; placing it in your mouth, tasting, swallowing and sensing it go down your throat. Pay attention only to the raisin. Despite the fact that so often we gobble down food, the act of eating just one raisin can help you focus on ONE THING and slow down your thinking. Taking another raisin can help you try again to practice staying aware and increase your vividness of experience."

The authors write that many people end up overweight because they are not aware of the satiation signals of their body. They assert that if people would eat more mindfully, they would be more aware of their body signals. An added benefit of eating mindfully is it can actually help you keep off the pounds!

In *The Mindful Way Through Depression,* they also outline the "healing power of awareness." They offer a step-by-step plan of other mindfulness practices and stress reduction techniques to help combat depression.

One of the co-authors of *The Mindful Way Through Depression,* Jon Kabat-Zinn, is the founding director of The Center for Mindfulness in Medicine, Health Care and Society at the University of Massachusetts Medical Center. Dr. Kabat-Zinn has been influential in making the practice of meditation more mainstream in Western society and his work has helped legitimize mind-body meditative practices in Western medicine and in educational settings.

In his book, *Wherever You Go, There You Are,* Kabat-Zinn writes,

"Mindfulness provides a simple but powerful route for getting ourselves unstuck, back in touch with our wisdom and vitality. It is a way to take charge of the direction and quality of our own lives, including our relationships within the family, our relationship to work and to the larger world and planet, and most fundamentally, our relationship with our self as a person."

Take a Moment for a
Mindfulness Activity

Gently close your eyes.

Be aware of any smells, sounds and sensations you are currently noticing.

Place your hands over your heart.

Relax your body and take three slow deep breaths.

Exhale slowly.

Release any tension in the body by gently massaging any tense areas.

Bring your awareness back to your breath.

As you breathe deeply, relax your muscles either progressively or all at one time.

Imagine your breath is a color, filling your body and then releasing into the air.

As you imagine the color leaving all parts of your body, breathe out any tension.

Breathe in compassion and peacefulness.

Visualize the rays of the sun beaming not only on you, but also inside of you, filling you with warmth of the rays.

Feel a renewed sense of energy emanating from within.

Slowly open your eyes, still mindful of the inner rays that glow from within.

Remind yourself that the gift of life is special, and so are you!

Do Your Wheels Need Alignment?

When we present seminars on personal balance we refer to a need to put ourselves into alignment. Just as a car needs occasional realignment of its tires to run smoothly and safely, at times we need to stop, take stock, and get rebalanced. In a spiritual sense, realigning yourself and balancing your physical needs with your spiritual needs will result in stopping long enough each day to acknowledge the magnificence of life itself. It will allow you to be filled with gratitude for the privilege of living.

Life is full of wonder, and so are we. Life is about continual growth, and the opportunity to move towards a sense of wholeness.

How about taking some "whole time"?

In "whole time" we let go of our judgmental self and embrace our nurturing self–it is a choice to heal and get mentally and emotionally centered. Remember your ability to learn from the past, dream of the future, and give yourself the gift of the present moment.

Beware of the Spirituality Deficiency Syndrome

Abraham Twerski, M.D., is both a Rabbi and a Psychiatrist, and is the founder of the Gateway Psychiatric Centers in Western Pennsylvania. He has written over 50 books on topics ranging from self-esteem, spirituality, addiction, and Jewish Theology. In his book, *Happiness and the Human Spirit: The Spirituality of Becoming the Best You Can Be,* he coins the phrase Spirituality Deficiency Syndrome (SDS) to describe modern day malaise. His premise is that despite the conveniences of modern life we often find ourselves looking outward for the satisfaction that can only come from within. Twerski is troubled by the prevalence of substance abuse and other types of addictive behavior, which offer quick fixes and temporary highs. Personal growth and pursuit of success become empty when spiritual growth is neglected. The modern advantage of having knowledge just a mouse click away does not always help us, but rather becomes a distraction from finding inner peace. He notes that many people find themselves afflicted with chronic discontent and fall short of the happiness they had imagined their success and even wealth would bring them. Thus, the materialism in our society, with the focus on quick fixes, has not necessarily correlated with happiness.

How can we find more spiritual fulfillment? Twerski believes that service and connectedness to others are vital for a meaningful life. Serve others, smile, extend a helping hand, give of yourself, and spread kindness.

As the saying goes: *Instead of keeping warm by wrapping yourself in a blanket, get warm by building a fire so that others can benefit from the heat as well.*

So clear your mind, nourish your soul!

"I will not let anyone walk through my mind with their dirty feet."

- Ghandi

HOW DO YOU SEE IT?

The Swiss Wiz says:

Opportunity is NOW HERE!

The Stinky Cheese says:

Opportunity is NO WHERE!

Opportunity is NOWHERE!

The view you take on life will determine your take on life!

In the words of
The Swiss Wiz...

- Waiting for tomorrow to be happy will get you nowhere!
- Being mindful of the present will help you heal and grow.
- Going through the holes in your life mindfully will help you become *whole*.
- Don't forget to *BE HERE NOW!*
- Watch out for the *Spiritual Deficiency Syndrome!* On the road to success, do not neglect your soul and do not neglect the importance of helping others along the way.

In the words of
The Swiss Cheese Fairy of Life...

- Let yourself be open to the warmth and love around you.
- Nourish yourself, slow down, and B-R-E-A-T-H-E!
- Pay attention to your needs for spirituality—filling your spirit can make you whole.
- Choose happiness and fulfillment now—you deserve it!
- You don't have to look far to be happy. Just look within yourself!

Swiss Cheese
Tool Kit

Assembling the Metaphorical Tool Kit

Do not underestimate the importance of spirituality and the gift of the present. All too often our time is spent anchored to yesterday or worrying and planning for tomorrow. Both the past and future are important in our lives, but don't let them steal precious moments from the HERE and NOW!

This ribbon will symbolize to you that today is a gift. Just like a ribbon that has been untied to reveal the present within, your life unfolds to allow you to experience and unleash life's beauty and joy!

> *Yesterday is history. Tomorrow is a mystery.*
> *Today is a gift. That is why they call it the present.*
> *- Eleanor Roosevelt*

Sixth Slice

Enjoy the Wine and Cheese Party!

Making People Connections

Enjoy the Wine and Cheese Party!
Making People Connections

🧀 *Do you find yourself too busy for your friends and family?*

🧀 *Do you ever talk to someone and then realize you have no idea what they just said?*

🧀 *Do you have at least one person to whom you can self-disclose?*

🧀 *Do you feel guilty when you say no?*

🧀 *Do people seem to take you the wrong way?*

🧀 *Do you allow conflict and anger to cloud your relationships with others?*

People need people! We are social creatures. Our level of happiness is often reflective of the quality of our close interpersonal relationships. That is precisely why communication skills are so important. If you can't express yourself freely, how will you be able to connect with others? On the other hand, if you express yourself freely with little concern for tact and sensitivity, your relationships will also suffer. Relationship problems and communication issues are among the main reasons why people seek counseling.

In this chapter, we will highlight the vital people skills that will enhance your relationships and improve your connection to others. We will offer guidelines on how to distinguish healthy from unhealthy communication. Make sure your people skills are not self-sabotaging! Even if you have to get out of your comfort zone, seek to expand your network of people connections, and take some risks by reaching out to others. This chapter will show you how to live by AT&T®'s former motto, "Reach out and touch someone!"

People Who Need People...

When you think of a wine and cheese party, what comes to mind? Sure, you might imagine cheese and cracker platters, with grapes sprinkled around the tray like a garnish. And of course, there might be wine glasses filled with all types of wine: blush, red, white, and rose. However, the wine and cheese are not really the main draw of the party.

The main attraction is PEOPLE. Steven Covey in *7 Habits of Highly Effective People* cites, *"Communication is the most important skill in life."* Noted speaker and author Zig Ziglar cites that 85 percent of a person's success depends on their relationship skills.

Yes, it is true. Our ability to make connections underlies our sense of well-being. It is the act of connecting with others and choosing camaraderie over isolation that softens the blows of the ups and downs of life, and enhances the thrills of true joy.

Did you ever hear Barbara Streisand's popular 60's song, *People?*

The first line goes, *"People, people who need people, are the luckiest people in the world."* Actually they are not really lucky–they are healthy. Luck implies that people skills are not something you need to work at. However, refining your interpersonal skills often takes conscious effort because connecting does not always come naturally. That's why we have reserved this chapter for focusing on the guidelines for healthy communication. People are social creatures. Those who deny that they need people, who isolate themselves for fear of getting hurt, are the ones who lose out. Some people think small talk is frivolous, or they might feel awkward not knowing what to say. The art of connecting is one of the most valuable skills in life. It is a vital component of emotional intelligence. Make it a point to connect with people regularly and expand your circle of friends–not shrink it!

"We might all be different,
but we do not need to be indifferent!"
- Judy Belmont

There's an "I" in Illness and a "We" in Wellness

Studies have shown that a sense of isolation and loneliness are part of the downward spiral of life dissatisfaction. Happiness has been significantly correlated to how connected you are and the strength of your relationships. Healthy relationships can actually lengthen your life! Countless studies have shown that people who live longer have at least one person to whom they can confide in.

Even being part of a group, such as a church, synagogue or social club can do wonders for your mental health. When we see clients, one of the first things we want to know is if they have a sense of belonging and if they feel connected. We have even suggested to clients to join a club, organization or place of worship–since a sense of belonging to something larger than yourself offers a forum of connection.

Ask the Therapist

Q: Are you saying I should join a church, even if I do not believe in God?

A: Throughout our years as therapists, we have seen many people find a sense of belonging through their place of worship. Getting closer to your spiritual self within a supportive community offers many intangibles that wealth, fame and fortune cannot buy. Of course, if you are turned off by organized religion, a church or temple might not be the place for you. Community outreach programs, or activities organized around events also help to heighten the experience of connectedness with others. Having a sense of community with others who share your interests, traditions, values and even hobbies can provide a feeling of social support.

"So long as we love, we serve; so long as we are loved by others,
I would almost say that we are indispensable; and no man is useless
while he has a friend."

- *Robert Louis Stevenson*

Even being part of a group, such as a church, synagogue or social club can do wonders for your mental health.

You Bring Yourself Wherever You Go

There is a story of a woman who went to her minister after moving with her family to a new community in a new city. She told the Reverend about how wonderful her church was in her former community, and how much she hoped she would have a sense of camaraderie in this new one. She told the Reverend of her volunteer efforts with the youth group, and her involvement with the church outreach committee. She smiled as she told him of the wonderful friends she met, and wanted to know if he felt she would find this same sense of community in this new church. Her minister replied, *"I think you will find the same thing here."*

The very next day, another woman went to the same minister after moving to the area with her own family. She told the Reverend about how glad she was to get away from her former church. She explained that she did not get involved in activities of the church since she felt like these organized activities ended up serving as forums for people to gossip. She viewed her fellow congregants as unfriendly and hypocritical. She had a falling out with a few people at the church, and still felt bitter about it. She explained to the minister that she was not treated well in her old church and wanted to know if he felt that it might happen again in the new church. Her minister replied, *"I think you will find the same thing here."*

This simple allegory highlights that it is not the place or the situation that defines your experience, but rather what you bring to the experience. The more you put in, the more you will get out of it. Things that bring meaning take effort, and by standing on the sidelines, you will feel distant and alienated. As Woody Allen said, "Eighty percent of success is showing up." So show up, get involved and you will see how well things turn out!

"The quality of your life is the quality of your relationships."
- Anthony Robbins

"A friend is one that knows you as you are, understands where you have been, accepts what you have become, and still, gently allows you to grow."
- William Shakespeare

Client Example:
A Place Does Not Define You

"I have no real way of meeting people. My office is small and I have nothing really in common with the few other women in the office. I wish we could move, but with my husband's job, we can't. I hate living in this area. We've lived here for 10 years and people have not been very friendly. I feel stuck and I find myself resenting him for keeping me away from my family."

Renee is not alone in thinking that her problems arise from being stuck in a particular place. She shares a common misconception that a location has the power to make you miserable. Sure, you can have preferences on where to live! However, there are miserable people even in Shangri-la! *You bring your attitude with you wherever you go! There are no geographic limitations on your attitude. It is your attitude that needs to be relocated!*

With this in mind, Renee began to join a network outside of work. She joined a Mom and Me class with her preschooler and began knitting with a group at a local yarn shop.

At first it was awkward at the Saturday morning knitting group. She felt self-conscious about going in alone, wondering, *"What am I doing here?"* Most of the women were older, and she had little in common with them aside from knitting. She was very glad she stuck with the class, since over time she found she had a lot in common with them, and also she ended up making some very strong friendships..

As Renee developed a sense of community, she no longer spent time focusing on her disappointments. She shifted from bemoaning her lot in life to creating a more satisfying and connected life.

"You can make more friends in two months by becoming interested in other people than you can in two years by trying to get other people interested in you."

- Dale Carnegie

Basic People Skills 101

An important ingredient in connecting with others is the quality of your communication style. There are the three main types of communication. The more you can identify and distinguish between the three general communication patterns, the more you will enjoy healthy relationships.

Below are the descriptions for the three styles of communication. Assertive communication is ideal because it is respectful and tactful. Aggressive or non-assertive communication digs you into a hole. Only assertive communication helps get you out of a hole–or helps you stay out in the first place!

Aggressive communication focuses on "you" statements, in which you express your rights honestly, but tactlessly, disregarding the feelings of others and showing a general lack of respect. Aggressive communication is designed to dominate, control, get back at, and prove how right you are. When you are aggressive, you violate the rights of others while you are standing up for your own. This grilled cheese type of behavior can be abrasive, angry or dismissive, as in the case of giving someone the cold shoulder.

Non-assertive communication sets you up to be resentful and misunderstood. Out of fear of disapproval, non-assertive people keep their thoughts to themselves and are pre-disposed to turn their anger inward or have their anger build up to erupt in an aggressive explosion. When you are non-assertive, people often take advantage of you as you acquiesce in order to avoid making waves. The cost of people-pleasing takes a toll on you when you live in fear of disapproval. This indirect, inhibited communication can lead to feelings of anxiety, sadness and isolation which contribute to psychosomatic problems that literally affect your health.

Assertive communication is the most ideal type of communication. It is characterized by "I" statements in which you express and assert your own rights, needs and desires. Acting assertively will lead to healthy relationships, in contrast to aggressiveness which tears relationships apart. Honesty, calmness and confidence underlie the assertive mindset, in which personal rights are embraced while the rights of others are respected. When you are assertive, you accept responsibility for your actions and do not blame others for making you feel a certain way. You do not feel a need to micromanage others to shape them into how you think they *should* be. Assertive communication demonstrates a healthy attitude about yourself and others.

> *Don't let your communication*
> *get you in a hole–let it get you out!*

"I" vs. "You" Statements

Assertive Communication uses "I" Statements

It is not selfish to use the word "I." It does not mean that you only care about yourself. Rather, "I" statements are direct, rational, objective and honest. "I" statements show that you are taking responsibility for how you feel and are not blaming someone else for your feelings. "I" statements are factual and non-judgmental.

Example: *"I felt bad when you said that to me in front of my friends. Please do not criticize me in front of them again."*

In that example, you ask for a change, tell the other person why you want a change, and will hope, but not expect, that you will win. Expressing yourself is the goal–not winning or getting your way.

Aggressive Communication uses "YOU" Statements

The word you is not a bad word, but when used to victimize, judge and control, it becomes an aggressive "you" statement. "You" statements are aggressive because the goal is to change someone else, whether it is their understanding, attitude or even their behavior. Ironically, "you" statements reflect more self-centeredness than "I" statements. Consider the same scenario as in the assertive example, but this time it is expressed in an aggressive way.

Example: *"You made me so mad in front of my friends!*
Never do that again!"

Do you notice how the blame is shifted to the other person for causing your feelings? Did you notice the commanding quality of the second statement? As you can see, aggressive statements are insensitive and judgmental. When you retaliate against what you think people are doing to you, you end up being the one who tries to control them! *It's called NAH, NAH, NAH, NAH, NAH, TIT FOR TAT!*

Did you ever wonder why people so out of control spend so much energy trying to control others?

Practicing "I" Messages

This is the formula for "I" messages:

I feel _____ when _____.

The Stinky Cheese likes "You" statements much better:

You made me feel _____ and you should have

_____.

Hopefully you prefer "I" statements over "You" statements!

"You" Statements	vs.	"I" Statement
You're not listening to me!		That is not what I meant.
That's impossible!		I'd be surprised if that happens.
It's just not practical.		I don't feel like it's practical.
You're never available!		I feel alone.
You always do this!		I do not like when you do this.
That's not true!		I don't agree with you.
You make me so mad!		I am angry when you do that.
You are a disappointment!		I don't appreciate your behavior.
What's wrong with you?		I am concerned about you.

Now it's your turn!

Turn these "You" messages into "I" messages.

YOU MESSAGE: *You make me so mad!*

I MESSAGE: _____

YOU MESSAGE: *You have no right to say that to me!*

I MESSAGE: _____

YOU MESSAGE: *You're much too sensitive.*

I MESSAGE: _____

CAUTION: Just because you start with I does not mean you are home free! Watch out for "you" statements disguised as "I" statements-such as "I think you stink!"

Change Yourself, Not OTHERS!

Why do people act aggressive? They want to change your:

- Mind
- Behavior
- Perception
- Way of doing things

Swiss can't turn into Muenster
And you can't change someone into someone they are not!

Are you a but head?
A *but* head is someone who uses *buts* to negate something they are saying. *Buts* devalue the positive intention. Try to make a positive statement out of a negative situation–if you start with yes and follow up with *but,* it negates the YES!

Replace "Yes, but" with "Yes if" or "Yes and"

Example:

"Yes, I like spending time with you, but not when you are rude to me."

Is changed into…
"Yes, I like spending time with you if you are respectful to me."

or

"Yes, I like spending time with you and look forward to spending more time with you when you are respectful."

Client Example:
The Duct Tape Worked!

"She has no idea how inane she sounds! Why should I treat her like a grown woman if she acts like a complete bimbo? This is not the woman that I married-she's become wacko! I could keep my cool if only she would start making some sense!"

Greg came into our first session with pages of examples of incidents, including the "dumb things my wife says" that he claimed were "*driving me crazy.*" His rage was quite apparent, and he made little attempt to conceal his resentment and anger by peppering his speech with rude and sarcastic comments. When I saw Greg and his wife in my office, his rude behavior bordered on verbal abuse and he would get visibly enraged. Over time, Greg learned to focus on choosing to have control over his reactions rather than defending himself. He said he learned how to successfully keep his reactions under wraps by using *The Duct Tape Rule.* Every time he got angry and was about to say something sarcastic and rude, he imagined that he had duct tape over his mouth. That visible image of the duct tape, he claimed, helped him save his marriage! During one session, he jokingly claimed, "I did not know that all I needed was just a little $1.99 duct tape to save my marriage! A divorce would have been much more costly than that!"

Watch How You are Saying It, Too!

It's not just what you say, but also how you say it! The importance of non-verbal communication is often overlooked. It is estimated that over 80% of communication is non-verbal. By focusing on what you say without noticing how you are saying things, you will be clueless about how you are coming across!

For example, giving someone the silent treatment gives off an unmistakable message without saying a word!

Consider this phrase:

I never said he stole the cheese!

Repeat this phrase seven times, emphasizing a different word each time. You will see that every time you stress a certain word, it means something completely different! This is a very convincing exercise that demonstrates the importance of tone and inflection on how you communicate.

Ask the Therapist

Q: My spouse and I keep arguing about little things, like who should put the laundry away or whose turn it is to take out the trash, and it always ends up in a big fight with both of us bringing up the garbage from the past! The strange thing is that a few days later we can't even remember what we were fighting about or how it started!

A: Did you ever hear of the "90/10 principle"? Ten percent of what we argue about is really about the topic at hand, like your spouse not taking out the trash. Ninety percent is our unresolved issues and expectations, past hurts, emotional baggage, and resentments from our past being played out in the present situation.

How do you get to the 90 percent?

- Give up the need to be right and to win.
- Stop and think before you speak.
- Let your guard down and stop being defensive.
- Refrain from being judgmental.
- Listen instead of reacting.
- Be empathetic to what the other person is feeling.

Look behind the obvious to listen and understand what is really going on. Don't get sidetracked! Examine the thoughts and feelings behind that 10 percent.

Another Rule of Thumb: If it won't matter 10 years from now, or even a year from now, maybe it does not need to matter so much now! This rule of thumb has a way of keeping things in perspective.

A Note for Parents

Many times, parents think it is okay to be aggressive with their children because they are the boss. Statements such as, "because I said so" and "while you're in my house, I get to make the rules," reflect an aggressive mentality which many parents consider acceptable. Although they mean well, this mentality leads to low self-esteem and rebellion in children. Instead of controlling your children, how about controlling yourself? Calmly setting limits and explaining the consequences of their behavior is assertive discipline–yelling, bossing, or pulling rank is not. In assertive discipline, children learn from natural and logical consequences.

NOTE:

- People who act in an authoritarian manner display aggressive behavior. The suffix -arian means "having the occupation of" and suggests rigidity.

- Authoritative communication is assertive. The suffix -ative means "tending towards" and suggests flexibility.

- No matter who you are communicating with, we urge you to strive for flexibility and rationality by acting in an authoritative rather than an authoritarian manner.

Just think - Much of the aggression and conflict in this world would be nonexistent if people learned as children the healthy habits of assertive behavior and not aggressive behavior, *where might makes right!*

The Stinky Cheese

thinks that if you feel angry, it's okay to show it! "I'm not going to hide my feelings!" Because of his anger, he does not realize that other people perceive him as abrasive. He does not realize he comes across like a piece of *sharp* cheddar!

The Swiss Wiz

knows that aggression is not a feeling, but a behavior. Just because you are feeling angry does not justify aggressive behavior–it will only hurt the other person, and yourself, in the long run! You have every right to feel angry, but you do not have the right to behave aggressively–that violates the rights of others.

The Swiss Cheese Fairy of Life

does not judge feelings–all feelings are okay, even angry ones. No feelings are unacceptable, but please be mindful of other's feelings. She realizes that when people are angry, they are feeling fragile. She understands how overwhelming emotions can be, and has faith in your ability to be gentle with yourself and others.

Don't get caught in the Chinese Finger Trap! This favorite carnival prize can teach us a lot about anger and conflict. Visualize yourself putting your fingers into the trap and pulling–this represents what happens in an argument. The more you pull, the tighter it gets and the more you are trapped. However, if you let go on one end and do not respond to the aggressive pulling from the other finger, you are set free and out of the trap. You can use the example of the Chinese Finger Trap as a reminder not to get caught up in a game of tit for tat, as you most certainly will find yourself stuck in the Chinese Finger Trap!

Use Active Listening

Hearing is passive–you don't need to exert effort to hear audible sounds.

Listening is active–it requires skills, interpretation and empathy.

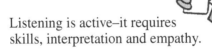

When people think of communication, they often think of talking, but good listening skills are just as important, and perhaps even more important!

In active listening, the focus is to validate rather than negate the other person's feelings. Active listening is a skill to use all the time, but particularly important to keep in mind during times of conflict. It is all too common to be on the defensive and explain or defend your position rather than affirm what the other person is saying. When you defend yourself and explain why you are right, you might not be open to what the other person is really saying. By summarizing and paraphrasing, rather than defending yourself, you can really listen to what other people are saying.

Remember: *The purpose of communication is to express–not impress. Active listening is focusing on the other person–not on yourself!*

The Stinky Cheese
does not use active listening.
He tells it like it is!

- Don't blame me.
- Why are you bringing that up again?
- I did not say that!
- You're not listening to me!

which leads to:

- A tendency to "talk at" rather than "talk to"
- Shutting the other person down
- Misunderstandings and misperceptions

The Swiss Wiz
knows the importance of using active listening.

- Sounds like you are very disappointed in me.
- I can see that you are really frustrated when I…
- Just to make sure I understand you, I think you might want me to…
- So what I hear you saying is…

which leads to:

- Validation of others.
- Empathy for others by showing warmth.
- An understanding of where others are coming from.
- Less of a tendency to assume, interpret and misjudge.

Putting your Assertiveness and Listening Skills to Work!

If you feel like you are in the hole of isolation and you need to crawl out, begin by listing ways that you can connect with others.

Here are some suggestions:

1. Make the effort to call someone, maybe even someone you haven't spoken to in a while.
2. Become more open to share your thoughts and feelings with close friends and family.
3. Be freer with compliments and words of appreciation for people close to you.
4. Make more time to get together with others, and take the first step!
5. Join activities and find people who share your interests and passions.

You can make it work!

If something does not work, try something else!

REMEMBER: Relationships can serve as a buffer against the stresses and strains of life. As we age, we need to keep connected rather than shrink our social circle. Meeting new friends or trying new activities can help us stay involved. You are never too old to connect and grow!

Watch What You Say, You Can't Take It Back!

There is a 19th century folktale about a man who went around town slandering the Rabbi. One day, he went to the Rabbi's home and asked for forgiveness. The Rabbi understood that this man had not realized the gravity of his transgressions, so he told him that he would forgive him on one condition: The man must return to his home, take a feather pillow from his house, cut it up, and scatter the feathers to the wind. After he had done this task, he was to come back.

Though puzzled by this strange request, the man was happy to be let off with so easy a penance. He quickly cut up the pillow, scattered the feathers, and returned to the house.

"Am I now forgiven?" he asked.

"Just one more thing," the Rabbi said.
"Go now and gather up all the feathers."

"But that's impossible. The wind has already scattered them."

"Precisely," the Rabbi answered. "And though you may truly wish to correct the evil you have done, it is as impossible to repair the damage done by your words as it is to recover the feathers. Your words are out there in the marketplace, spreading hate, even as we speak."

How quick we are to speak without thinking of the effect our words will have on others. Especially in times of stress, we often speak our minds carelessly, caught in the emotion of the moment. It is so easy to believe the bad things that people say about others, so easy to accept the news that we hear in the media or read in tabloids, that we act ready to assume the role of critic and judge.

"A bird that you set free may be caught again, but a word that escapes your lips will not return."
- Jewish proverb

"We might not have it all together, but together we have it all!"
- Unknown

In the words of
The Swiss Wiz...

- Communication is important in everything we do!

- There are three types of communication: assertive, non-assertive and aggressive.

- The goal of assertive behavior is to express yourself, not to get what you want.

- Active listening is not only hearing–it requires effort and shows empathy.

- Watch what you say–you can't take it back.

- It's not just what you say, it's how you say it!

In the words of
The Swiss Cheese
Fairy of Life...

- Say what you think and feel, as long as it is respectful to others.

- It feels good to belong–communicate and don't isolate yourself.

- Let yourself be part of something larger than yourself–you will feel more whole.

- Please, open your heart and let people in.

- Have faith in yourself. People will love you–they just need to meet you!

The Swiss Cheese
Tool Kit

Assembling the Metaphorical Tool Kit

Anyone for a game of cards? No matter what type of card game you play, you often use the whole deck. Most people find it more fun to play card games with others rather than playing solitaire. There are many cards in the deck and they are all necessary. Sure, some seem better than others, like the ace or king, but in the game of poker, a king won't do any good if someone has a full house of fives and threes. In this scenario, the three and five are both more valuable than the king. The deck of cards reminds us that we need all of the cards in the deck, just like we need all types of people in this world. We need to work together to make a full deck. And don't throw out the Joker! It might be a little careless and wild, but it reminds us to not take ourselves too seriously.

Like the deck of cards, we need all types of people to make our experiences successful. Learn from one another, enjoy your differences and gain support, commonality, and connections through your friendships. Everyone is unique, just like each card is in a deck of cards. All of us have cards we are dealt in life, but how you play your hand is up to you, and that will determine if you have a shot at being a winner!

Seventh Slice

Cheese Lite!

Welcoming Wellness for a Healthier You!

Cheese Lite!

Welcoming Wellness for a Healthier You!

 *Do you think about exercising and then just let those thoughts disappear?*

 *Are you always planning to start eating healthier tomorrow?*

 *Do you promise yourself that tonight you will get a good night's rest, yet end up watching the late, late show?*

 *Do you feel like you don't have enough spunk, energy or laughter in your daily life?*

If you want to welcome wellness into your life, then doing things that are healthier for you on a daily basis offers the key to unlocking the door for a better life. People often envy those who seem to have it all, but it is so much more productive to focus on appreciating the steps you are taking to improve your *own* life. Know that you can make the transition to a healthier lifestyle right now. Even small steps can get you to your goal as long as you keep on moving forward. To implement the wellness tips in this chapter, begin by taking an inventory of what you want in your wellness lifestyle and what habits need to go!

Bring the awareness of the importance of wellness into your daily life. Sample a taste of an exciting life that awaits you if you take charge of your health–so take a small bite and begin today. Do this for life–your life!

"My doctor told me to keep in shape.
Well, this is my shape and I'm keeping it!"

Jack LaLanne, "The Godfather of Fitness," was one of the first people to recognize and successfully communicate to the public the importance of exercise and nutrition. Wellness, good health and longevity were his passions and have spanned more than a half a century. In the early 1950's, he launched his first television show which ran for thirty years. He also began the first health club in the mid 1930's, which eventually grew to over 200 clubs in the U.S. (Jack LaLanne gyms became Bally Total Fitness™ in the mid 1980's). During his eighty year career, he taught by example and shared his tips with others. It seems safe to say that Jack LaLanne held the secrets to being healthy. He emphasizes that to live a long life of wellness, each person has to make health and fitness a part of their daily living. As LaLanne explained, "It has to become a habit just like anything else."

When you are not active you have less muscle and more fat. A pound of fat burns two calories a day. A pound of muscle burns 30-50 calories a day. It's a no brainer; even I can do the math! Now I just have to do the rest by being active.

I am trying to convert my calories into usable energy. Now that I know that my metabolism will actually speed up even after I am finished exercising, I realize that instead of storing my fat I can build muscle.

Keeping in shape is about movement and movement means leaving behind coach potato thinking…and the potato chips. It is a no ifs, ands, or buts way of handling your daily lifestyle. Translation: Get up and get moving!

Drs. Michael Roizen and Mehmet Oz, in their best-selling book, *YOU, Being Beautiful,* write that when it comes to cardiovascular exercise and stamina training, begin by walking 30 minutes a day (of course, speak with your doctor before beginning any exercise program). Then find ways to "break a sweat a few days a week to improve your cardiovascular health." This can be achieved through numerous activities such as running, tennis, biking, hiking, aerobic classes, dancing, boxing, rollerblading or swimming. Just make exercise a habit!

Consider this...
The Stinky Cheese says:

- I'm too busy, I hardly have enough time in the day to do what I need to do, and besides, I don't even like to exercise! My day is already so full!

- I have no energy to exercise! I am tired and run down, how will I ever get the energy to work out?

- I am just not motivated. After all, is it really going to make a difference? I will probably just quit in a few weeks anyway, so why bother starting? Exercise just isn't my thing.

- I am not athletic, besides I am afraid I might hurt myself in the process and then what will happen? Maybe I don't have the skills I need–after all, I have never been athletic!

- I don't have enough money to join a gym or hire a personal trainer like some other people do. It just costs way too much money to stay in shape!

And then consider this…
The Swiss Wiz
cautions about having this type of "Stinky Thinking"!

He says:

Find some form of exercise that feels like fun to you! Find a time to fit it in your schedule on a regular basis. Are you a morning person? Then do it first thing in the morning. If after work is the best time, don't stop at home, go right to it!

- Although exercising takes energy to do, once you exercise regularly you will have even more energy!

- Change your self-talk. You don't have to love exercising. Just make a list of your reasons for getting in shape and commit to your goals–add new activities for more enjoyment.

- The desire to be fit is a mindset that is in your control. Take classes, practice, and make fitness as important as other things you do in your life!

- Consider all the options, like low cost DVD's, on-demand exercise programs, walking, taking the stairs, and weight-training. Ask for birthday and holiday fitness gift certificates. Make it a part of your budget and don't forget to check out your company/medical reimbursements for fitness related activities.

NO Ifs, Ands, or Butts

Just a 15-minute walk twice a day burns an extra 100 calories daily. You can feel lighter and lose five pounds in just six months, even if you continue eating the same amount, simply by adding this small amount of exercise.

Try wearing a pedometer to track your mileage–studies show that people walk farther when wearing a pedometer. It can be very reinforcing to see how far you walk!

Pick one or more activities on the following page and try incorporating something new into your life and lighten your load.

- Fitness experts suggest that you get a mix of cardiovascular exercise, strength training and stretching to help with flexibility.

- Remember, muscle burns more calories than fat!

- Write down your fitness goals and keep a daily log to help get the best results.

- Enjoy a workout with a friend, join a local gym, or consider being part of a hiking, running or biking group–get fit while you make new friends and have fun with old ones.

- Fit exercise into your weekly schedule; write it in your schedule like all your other appointments.

"Lack of activity destroys the good condition of every human being, while movement and methodical physical exercise save it and preserve it."

- Plato

How many calories are you burning?

Activity	Calories burned in 15 minutes
Aerobic dance	170
Basketball	140
Bicycling at 12 mph	140
Bicycling at 15 mph	180
Bicycling at 18 mph	210
Circuit weight training	190
Cross-country skiing	145
Downhill skiing	105
Golf (carrying clubs)	90
In-line skating	150
Jumping rope, 60-80 skips/min	140
Karate, Tae Kwon Do	190
Kayaking	75
Racquetball	115
Rowing machine	105
Running, 10-minute miles	180
Running, 8-minute miles	220
Ski machine	140
Slide	150
Swimming freestyle, 35 yd/min	125
Swimming freestyle, 50 yd/min	130
Tennis, singles	115
Tennis, doubles	40
Stair climber	190
Walking, 15-minute miles, level	70
Water aerobics	70

Calorie Chart: 3500 calories equals a pound.

Weighty Issues

We have an epidemic in this country. According to medical experts, obesity is becoming the number one health-related issue in the U.S. Over 300,000 deaths each year are related to obesity, second only to cigarette smoking. People who are overweight are more prone to breathing problems, Type II Diabetes, stroke, heart disease, certain types of cancer, psychological disorders such as depression, anxiety, and sleep problems. Despite the accessibility of low fat foods, childhood obesity has doubled in the last 30 years and overweight children have a much higher risk of turning into overweight adults.

The Good News is...

- Losing five-to-ten percent of your excess body weight can reduce your risk factors for heart disease and may provide other health benefits.

- You will feel better, have more energy and be in better shape!

- Making health a priority will have a positive impact on your life.

- Making healthy food choices is a good habit to get into, which is a vital component of welcoming wellness in your life.

- Being a healthy eater will influence those you live with, and might inspire others to change their eating habits.

New York Times best-selling author, Don Colbert, M.D., emphasizes in his book, *Eat This and Live!* how important it is for kids to eat healthy. "One of the easiest ways to get your kids to try new foods is to get them involved in the grocery store. Let them be in charge of picking out one new fruit or vegetable a week. Teach them to read food labels and make a game out of finding the healthiest bread, pasta, or cereal product. At home, make kids part of meal preparation..."

Tips and Tools for a Fit Life!

"I am trying to eat healthy, but everything is better with butter. I am having a sugar attack and I don't exactly have the desire to eat a hunk of lettuce instead! Help! I need a food makeover!"

Use less fats, sugars and carbohydrates!

Limit your fat intake to no more than 30 percent of your total caloric intake. There are healthy monounsaturated fats which are found in extra virgin olive oil (or EVOO as Rachael Ray calls it); they are also in peanut butter and nuts–especially almonds. Omega-3 fats are also healthy fats with anti-inflammatory properties that may lower your blood pressure and reduce the risk of stroke, heart attacks and blood clots. Omega-3 fatty acids are found in fatty fish like wild salmon, and are also found in flaxseed.

Suggestion: Include 90 grams of lean protein in your daily meals and snacks. It helps keep you full longer. Protein can be found in dairy, meat, and poultry, as well as beans and legumes.

Guidelines from the Centers for Disease Control (www.cdc.gov/nutrition/everyone) suggest preparing food and beverages with few added sugars. Major sources of added sugar in our daily diet include regular soft drinks, candy, cake, cookies, pies, and fruit drinks. Sugar may be listed in many different ways such as brown sugar, corn syrup, glucose, sucrose, honey, and molasses. How about trying a novel way of reducing your sugar level? A new study from Sweden shows that just one teaspoon of cinnamon a day can lower blood sugar levels.

> *"Life itself is the proper binge."*
> *- Julia Child*

With this economy, everyone is downsizing and I have decided to do the same for my body. I am eating lighter and I feel like my carbon footprint is less bloated. Stop recycling your old thoughts about your food habits and fall in love with fruits and vegetables; they are so much more colorful than butter anyway. Get with the program–*fit is in!*

Eat more fruits, vegetables, whole grains, and fiber.

Have five servings a day of fruits and vegetables. They have antioxidants which help prevent chronic diseases and they are high in fiber which may reduce the risk of certain types of cancer. Gradually add more fiber to your daily menu and drink lots of water.

Smart Snacking
- Bananas: Loaded with potassium and B6
- Blueberries: High in antioxidants
- Rice crackers: Low in calories and so many different flavors!
- Apples: Vitamin C
- Low or reduced-fat cheese: Good source of calcium
- Low-fat yogurt with fruit: Fiber and calcium
- Unbuttered and unsalted air popcorn: Low in fat, high in fiber
- Vegetables with dip/low-fat yogurt: Loaded with vitamins and low in fat
- Grapes, watermelon, cantaloupe: Low in fat and naturally sweet
- Apple slices with peanut butter: Fiber and healthy fats
- Nuts: Healthy natural food with lots of protein
- Baked whole-grain chips with salsa: Fiber from the chips and lycopene from the tomatoes (which may help prevent prostate cancer)
- Whole-grain cereal with low-fat milk: High in fiber and calcium

Food for Thought!

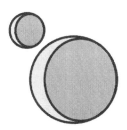

The holes in the Swiss cheese have no calories!
Go ahead, help yourself to some!

Water: Many times people think they are hungry when they are really thirsty. Drinking water will fill you up and quench your thirst. People who lower their consumption of sugar-laden soft drinks by three a day have the potential to lose over 10 pounds in a year. Water is one of the best things in life and it is actually cheap. Drink at least 7 eight-ounce glasses of water or other sugar-free liquids a day. Here's how to know if you are hydrated: If your urine is clear or pale yellow, you are probably getting enough fluids.

Ask yourself if you are feeling BAD–Bored, Angry or Depressed. These emotions are common reasons for overeating!

Cravings fast fact: You know you're not really hungry, but you have these cravings to just eat anything in sight. Wait at least five minutes before giving in to your cravings. Many times cravings actually pass once we decide whether or not we are going to act on our impulses. Instead, take out a pen and a piece of paper and write down what you are feeling. If it is not physical hunger, ask yourself if you are really just feeling BAD: Bored, Angry, Depressed? If you are psychologically hungry, think of what is really going on and take action. Even just going outside for a walk can be a good distraction and a way to lighten your load, easing the thoughts that are coming from your mind while moving your behind!

How about keeping a food/mood/thought diary? When you feel the urge to emotionally eat, pinpoint your feelings and the thoughts that underlie those feelings. This can help you get to the root of the issue without eating your way through it!

More Food for Thought!

- Remember to give yourself fuel at the start of the day–don't let your energy level tank.
- Don't skip meals.
- Fast fact: Not eating for more than three hours can lead to a drop in blood sugar levels, which causes weakness and fatigue. So eat smaller, more frequent snacks and meals.
- Breakfast fast fact: Eating a fiber-rich cereal for breakfast can reduce fatigue by 10 percent, improve cognitive skills and lessen feelings of the blues.
- Eat a variety of foods. No foods have to be off limits if you exercise portion control.
- Slice it or dice it! Did you know that one serving of cheese (or two ounces) is equivalent to eight pieces of diced cheese? Make chunks into smaller pieces that take more time to eat, and seem like more!
- Moderate amounts of alcohol with your cheese can be part of a healthy lifestyle, but don't go overboard!

Alcohol fast fact: Alcohol is high in calories and sugars. It is also low in nutritional minerals and vitamins. Alcohol lowers your inhibitions which can lead to overeating or binge eating. Heavy use of alcohol has been linked to liver cancer and even cancer of the mouth, throat and esophagus. Women who consume a few drinks a day may also increase their risk of breast cancer. If you do drink, do so in moderation and seek help if you feel your drinking habits are not in moderation. Studies do suggest that red wine in moderation can be good for you. It is high in polyphenols, a type of anti-oxidant found in fruits skins that may reduce health problems such as cancer and heart disease. As with any food or drink, moderation is the key.

"The second day of a diet is always easier than the first. By the second day you're off of it."
- Jackie Gleason

"My doctor told me to stop having intimate dinners for four, unless there are three other people."
- Orson Welles

CheeZZZ's-Sleep!
Universal among all human beings is the need for sleep.

So how are your sleep habits?

Do you say that you are going to go to bed at a reasonable time, but still find yourself up at 1 a.m. surfing the internet or watching TV?

Are you in bed tossing and turning, or waking up several times a night?

Do you sleep less than six hours a night?

Effects of not getting enough sleep (less than six hours):

- An increase in pain and a decrease in immune function.
- Decrease in cognitive function and reasoning.
- Behavior is more likely to be irritable, easier to anger.
- Decrease in energy level.
- Mood is more depressed.
- The stress hormone, cortisol, is released in the body causing our bodies to not let go of excess weight, especially around the midsection.
- Encourages an increase in appetite as it affects hormones that control our desire to eat more.

"It is a common experience that a problem difficult at night is resolved in the morning after the committee of sleep has worked on it."
- John Steinbeck

"Fatigue is the best pillow."
- Benjamin Franklin

Extra! Extra!

Too much sleep is not so good either. As with food and exercise, moderation is the key!

In his sleep lab at UC San Diego Medical Center, Daniel F. Kripke, M.D., found that although it is a common belief that eight hours a night is an optimal amount of sleep, people who lived longer only averaged six to seven hours a night. His studies showed that those who slept less than four hours per night or more than eight hours had significantly increased mortality rates compared to those who slept six to seven hours. The best survival rates were in the group that averaged seven hours of sleep.

"Sleep is the best meditation."
– Dalai Lama

Give yourself the gift of rest and relaxation. All too often we focus on nurturing others and neglect ourselves. Make it a priority to refresh yourself so you can feel as good as you deserve to be!

There is no right amount of sleep for everybody. Listen to your body and do not pressure yourself by thinking you have to get a certain amount of sleep. Reading a book or doing a quiet activity if you can't sleep will certainly be no tragedy! At some points in our lives we need more sleep, so please, be flexible! We all have an ideal set point of sleep that is unique to our own bodies.

Client Example:
Help! I've fallen,
but not to sleep!

Lora

Sally was an educated and attractive woman in her 50s that came into my office saying that she was having trouble sleeping. She felt that she couldn't concentrate, had no energy, was irritable with her twin girls and quick to anger towards her husband. Her medical doctor had ruled out any physical causes and prescribed her a low dose of a prescription sleep medication to help her fall asleep. Sally said she was hesitant to take the medication, but she felt like it was her only option to re-gaining her sanity. She said that the medication did help her fall asleep, but the next morning her daughter noticed a pile of eggshells in the trash–Sally had made herself a six egg omelet with cheese (being professional, I did not ask her what type of cheese was in the omelet). Sally was horrified to see that she had an unusual side effect of her medication referred to as "sleep eating." She described her life as happy and satisfying before having this sleep problem for the last three months. There was nothing that was troubling her, except her lack of sleep.

We set up a routine to get her in the habit of getting good quality sleep; increasing her effective coping skills and energy level. She started going to bed and getting up at the same time each day. She stopped eating or drinking two hours before bed and she did not watch TV in bed anymore. She lowered the temperature in her bedroom. Sally also stopped drinking caffeinated drinks after 3 p.m. and started exercising regularly, which also helped her get a good night's rest. Before bedtime, she started a ritual of soaking in the tub with candles glowing and soothing music, which helped relax her mind and body. Sally is now sleeping seven to eight hours a night, has renewed energy and is able to enjoy her family, her work and her life. Small changes and big results!

Think of an activity that lowers your blood pressure and heart rate, enhances your immune system, releases pain fighting hormones in the body, doesn't cost any money and reduces muscle tension better than a massage! No, we are not talking about sex, but that is a very good guess. We are talking about...

Laughter

Laughter helps you get out of a dark hole or over a distressing event and it gives you the ability to see the "lite" side of things. Throughout this book we have encouraged you to look at life like Swiss cheese. Sure, there will be holes and it's important to acknowledge the holes and get through them. Yet all too often, people disregard laughter–humor is vital to weather the holes in life that seem like ditches or craters. As psychotherapists, we work with our clients to balance seriousness with using humor to LIGHTEN UP and not take things so seriously! Have you ever heard of Laughing Cow® Swiss cheese? It is Swiss without the holes. No wonder it is laughing! In the Laughing Cow® ads they ask, *"Have you laughed today?"*

Well, have you laughed today?

Laughter really is good medicine–it causes a release of feel-good chemicals called endorphins. *Medical experts say that you can get laughter without a prescription!* So fill up on your daily dose of laughter and remember, don't take life too seriously; after all, no one gets out of here alive!

Laughter isn't really a habit, but we would like to make it one!

"The most wasted of all days is one without laughter."
- E.E. Cummings

In his best-selling book, *The 100 Simple Secrets of Happy People,* author David Niven, Ph.D., cites hundreds of studies showing that happiness and laughter are related. Being able to laugh at a good joke, or at life itself, is a real source of satisfaction in life. It's a "gut-level" fact that people who enjoy humor are more likely to feel happy.

Ways To Laugh More

- Be around people who make you laugh, smile or are just plain silly. (There are no age limits, they can be as young or as old as you like.)
- Hang around your pets and discover their humorous ways.
- See the humor in the absurd, as sometimes you can really crack yourself up.
- Go to a comedy club or watch a funny movie.
- Cut out funny pictures and put them up at work or around the house to share with others.
- Read a funny book.
- Ask people to email you funny articles and humorous pictures.
- Smile more often; and people will often smile with you–it's contagious!

"In the course of my life, I have often had to eat my words, and I must confess that I have always found it a wholesome diet."
- Winston Churchill

In the words of
The Swiss Wiz...

- Commit to becoming the best and healthiest you!
- Setting goals for your health and fitness turn obstacles into opportunities for success.
- Sleep well, eat right and laugh more!
- Find outlets for exercise that work for you–and stick with it!
- Don't allow negative self-talk to stop you if you have a setback. Keep right on going!
- Enhance your energy level with good health habits!

In the words of
The Swiss Cheese
Fairy of Life...

- Realize that you can live your best life today and everyday!
- Laugh often and look at your life "lite-ly."
- Welcome wellness with open arms and give yourself the gift of a healthy and happy heart.
- Take care of yourself–no one else has the ability to do that like you can!
- Each step you take to take care of your body is a step towards loving yourself.

Swiss Cheese
Toolkit

Assembling the Metaphorical Tool Kit

Cheese Lite is all about letting go of old habits or ways of thinking and beginning to lighten up.

The bubbles represent a way for you to think about lightening up your day in a number of ways. Think about how much fun children have just blowing bubbles. Do you ever blow bubbles? It is like skipping; you just can't feel sad and skip at the same time. Try it!

Get in the habit of laughing. Can you think of something funny or amusing right now? So laugh and be bubbly and bring joy to your life. Enjoy!

The good news about the holes in Swiss cheese is that they have absolutely no calories, take no energy to lift and you can see right through them–they are as light as bubbles. So take some weight off your mind and remind yourself that you can get through the holes of your life with an attitude of levity and a large dose of healthy living!

> *"He, who has health, has hope.*
> *And he who has hope has everything."*
> *- Ralph Waldo Emerson*

Eighth Slice

The Cheese Wheel of Life - How Do You Slice It?

Achieving Life Balance

The Cheese Wheel of Life - How Do You Slice It?

Achieving Life Balance

Are you spread way too thin?

Do you find that you don't have the time to do the things you want to?

Do you find it hard to motivate yourself and get things done?

Do you fantasize about leaving everything behind and starting all over in another city, state or planet?

Do you have trouble turning off the day and enjoying your nights?

Are you taking on more tasks and responsibilities, but enjoying them less?

In this chapter, we'll look at where and how you divide your time and energy. How do you slice your life's wheel? Do you serve up way too many slices in one realm of your life, such as your work, leaving very few slices for your spouse, family, close friends…and even yourself? In your quest to be everything to everybody, have you left yourself spread so thin that you feel like you are losing perspective and find that you have less time and energy in your daily life? If you feel, at times, like your life is out of balance, step back and look at how you are spending your mental and physical energy. Some days you cannot help but be overly-focused on one thing or another, but the key is to let yourself regroup and reprioritize how you spend your time. You don't need to be Superman or Superwoman, although it might be tempting to try! Just remember, if you spend too many days out of balance, something has to give and it might be your physical and emotional health, along with your peace of mind.

Are You Sliced Too Thin?

Just take this simple 5-minute quiz and find out if you are indeed sliced too thin. For each question, circle either Yes or No.

1. When you are at home, do you find yourself thinking about work a great deal of the time? **Yes No**

2. Are you spending too much time at your workplace, even though you promise yourself you are going to leave earlier? **Yes No**

3. Are you too tired after work to take care of yourself or enjoy your time with friends or family? **Yes No**

4. Do people close to you seem like a source of irritation or frustration? **Yes No**

5. When you go to bed at the end of the day, do you feel like you didn't have enough time to do the things you wanted to do? **Yes No**

6. Are you spending too little time with those you love? **Yes No**

7. Is your time being taken up by too many emails, phone calls, and errands that you don't enjoy? **Yes No**

8. Are those close to you unhappy because you are unavailable to them most of the time? **Yes No**

9. Are you overwhelmed with the feeling that you have too much to do and never enough time? **Yes No**

10. Do you find yourself trying to be everything to everyone? **Yes No**

Add up your yes responses and compare with the answer key to see if you are slicing yourself too thin.

0-2 Yes responses: *You have a wholesome balance.*

3-6 Yes responses: *You are trying to balance, but you might be a few steps away from slipping into the hole.*

7-10 Yes responses: *Ok, so now realize you are in the work/life hole. If you put your mind to it, you don't have to stay there.*

If you feel like you are in the hole, realize that you have the opportunity every day to get through it! Imagine yourself stepping up on a ladder and seeing things from a different perspective, but don't lose your balance!

Many of us spend our lives in a frenzy with thoughts that might sound like this, "One day I will be able to have a balanced life...when the kids are gone, when I work part-time, when I retire, when I move." But more often than not, that day never comes–and when, or if, it comes we still haven't learned the skills needed to appreciate that is has arrived.

If we don't learn the skills that are necessary to balance what we need and what we want right now, how can we assume that we'll learn them at a later date? Some of us think we will balance our lives after we accomplish something great. In fact, a great person who did accomplish great things said...

"I long to accomplish a great and noble task, but it is my chief duty to accomplish small tasks as if they were great and noble."
- *Helen Keller*

Don't Go Off the Ledge - Reclaim Your Wedge!

Finding and keeping your balance is about knowing how to make the right cut, at the right time, in the right proportion…for you!

If we look at a wheel of Swiss cheese, the wedges of cheese that we slice may end up in disproportionate wedges–but they are still parts of the whole wheel. In our daily life, we only get 24 hours in the day. How much we have to give to others and to ourselves will depend on how we choose to spend our time. Slices may come in different sizes and we have the opportunity to make the way we slice our various tasks and commitments work for us. Despite the huge variation in how we focus our time, we often find it a struggle to have the right amount of slices in the correct proportion to satisfy our taste. The way we divide our time might look quite different.

Try it! Make two circles and in one, show the various slices of how you divide your time between things like work, hobbies, relaxation, getting together with friends, spending time with family, paying bills and doing other household chores, etc. In the other circle, show how you would ideally like to slice things. If the actual and the ideal are far apart, how can you make changes to be closer to your ideal? The more time spent catering to the needs, wants and desires of others, the more you will find yourself becoming like bleu cheese. If you are spread too thin, you are not taking good enough care of yourself if you fail to balance your life.

I don't need to be blue-I will decide what I want and need to do, not only for you and you, but me too!

"Don't let time divide you, learn to divide your time and energy in a way that makes you feel balanced."

- Judy Belmont

There is no vaccination against negativity.

Don't be afraid of catching negativity–concentrate on emanating positive energy to others and they may catch it!

Positive people do positive things–and balancing their priorities is one of them. When you focus on prioritizing what is important to you, you are more likely to feel in balance instead of unbalanced.

Singer Rod Stewart's song, *"Every Picture Tells a Story,"* could be applied to the issue of life balance. Look at your picture; if it is not what you want it to be, you are responsible for changing the picture and changing the story!

**"Can you vaccinate me against negativity?
Everyone at work has it and I'm afraid I'll catch it!"**

Picture This!

Take a really good look and see how you can rewrite your own story or draw your own picture. What do you need to do to change the picture? Whether it is the words we speak, the way we carry ourselves, our beliefs about ourselves, the smile or frown on our face, or the way we spend our time, they all tell a story. In other words, live your life the way you picture a balanced life. What do you need/want to see in that picture?

Take time to reflect and give yourself some quiet time to ask yourself these questions and then listen for the answers.

- What do you want to see in this picture?
- How can you frame it to look like something that you want?
- What do you need to do to get your slice?
- What slices are you willing to give to others?
- Who can help you with this picture?
- How will you know if your life is balanced the way you pictured it to be?

In order to feel as though your life is in sync, be aware and pay attention to how you choose to live your life on a daily basis. Look at how you carve time for yourself, whether at home or at work. Are you cutting anything out of your life that you need for creating harmony and balance?

Time, like money, is a commodity…and one of the best investments you can ever make is to invest in yourself by devoting the time to create a balanced and wholesome life.

Make sure when you divide your time that you give yourself plenty of leeway to balance yourself. It's okay to get off track sometimes if you learn from it and right yourself, change direction and shift your priorities. Achieving balance in life requires a lot of flexibility, and giving yourself enough space to shift direction and change your mind is vital. Different things work for us at different times. The balancing act is never done– that's what makes us grow and become so distinctive like a good piece of holey Swiss!

Client Example:
Balancing does not mean escaping!

Terry felt like her life was spinning out of control. She felt a lack of support from her husband and started to withdraw emotionally after one particularly bad argument. As a full-time working mom, her late afternoon and evening hours were largely spent tending to the needs of her children while her husband worked second shift. Feeling sorry for herself, and feeling like her life was completely out of whack, she started drinking with her neighbors most nights after her children went to sleep. The more she drank, the more she felt like she was getting something for herself. The excessive drinking led to more marital problems, until she ended up getting a wake-up call when her husband left her after he found out that she became intimate with one of her friend's husbands while they were drinking one night.

In counseling, Terry learned to differentiate between nurturing herself with good self-care habits and escaping from her pain and resentment through partying and excessive alcohol use. She stopped looking to alcohol as a way to anesthetize her pain and frustration. Both Terry and her husband learned to improve their communication, and became more insightful and supportive of one another.

As they became more balanced individually, they achieved a much healthier balance as a couple. The erratic and impulsive behaviors were replaced with more mature and responsible choices.

*"Nothing is particularly hard
if you divide it into small jobs."*
- Henry Ford

Julie Morgenstern's book, **Never Check E-mail in the Morning,** *helps her readers prioritize and organize their lives to unleash energy and potential. The following are some excerpts from the best-selling author:*

"Consider that your perceptions might be off. Working harder and longer than anyone else doesn't mean you're operating at peak productivity."

"Focus. When you are at work, really concentrate; take no calls on family matters unless it's an emergency. And when you're with your kids, let your answering machine take messages. Compartmentalize so that whatever you're doing, you're giving it your all."

"Set a two-hour wrap-up alarm on your computer, beeper, cell phone. This will help you focus on your upcoming exit time, and will force you to finish up what you are doing without starting one more big project or call."

"Plan something time sensitive immediately after work. Take a class, meet a friend for dinner, or have a particular train or car pool to meet. A non-negotiable deadline will get you out the door on time."

"Get a buddy at work that will leave with you. You'll motivate each other to get out on time. If that buddy happens to have as big a sense of duty as you do, all the better!"

"Think of creating a personal life as an investment in your work. If you are refreshed and balanced, you will have more energy to be more productive. If you feel uncomfortable taking time for yourself, do it for your clients, boss, and colleagues."

> *"The hardest part is getting started."*
> *- J.C. Penney*

With so many choices in the wheel of life, it is helpful to begin by asking these questions:

Am I making the most of today? What am I afraid will happen if I do things differently? Are my fears real or imagined? How can I turn fear into courage? What am I grateful for when I wake up in the morning? How tolerant am I when it comes to me or others? Am I open and willing to look at things in another way? How willing am I to go through transitions and look at all new beginnings as possibilities for a better and more balanced life?

Ask yourself, "Who do you most admire that is resilient and balanced?" Chances are, this individual has a high degree of maturity, confidence, and trust in their inner voice.

The Swiss Wiz says:

- Slow down and stop in order to appreciate what is really important to you.
- Ask yourself: What is the best use of my time now?
- You can make better choices for yourself if you are more in touch with what you want to do rather than what you have to do.
- Make each moment count, instead of counting the moments.

"Life is a succession of moments. To live each one is to succeed."
– Coretta Scott King

"Life is like riding a bicycle.
To keep your balance, you must keep moving."
– Albert Einstein

Throughout the day check-in with yourself...

- Am I getting the most out of the time I have right now?
- On what slices of my life am I spending too much time and what slices need more of my time?
- What slices do I want to enhance? Am I using my energy in the way that is healthiest for me?
- What parts of the puzzle can I fit into my day?

"I'm working so hard at my time management skills that it leaves me little time to get anything else done."

— *Anonymous*

One thing at a time: The new approach to multi-tasking and balance

You can always make plans and think about the future. But, the only time it ever is…is now. So the time to focus on your work/life balance is the present! Balance involves planning for the future, and being open to life NOW!

In gym class, you may have tried walking on a balance beam. In order to stay balanced, you needed to walk steadily on that beam, securely and carefully, with one foot after another. When we multi-task, we often lose sight of what it means to be present, to do one thing at a time, and really be open to the experience.

In her book, *One Thing at a Time: 100 Simple Ways to Live Clutter-Free Every Day,* Cindy Glovinsky writes that to avoid feeling like obstacles will stop or deter you, keep repeating to yourself the mantra "one thing at a time." Similar to the popular phrase in AA–"one day at a time," this simple phrase serves as a reminder to take it easy and not to get ahead of yourself. When you feel overwhelmed you can stay the course by not jumping ahead and worrying about everything there is to do, but rather focus on the steps you are doing now to "get there." Slowing yourself down helps you feel centered as well as empowered.

Despite all of our conveniences, advanced technology along with all the appliances and electronics that provide help in our daily lives, we find ourselves more stressed and busier than ever. We have more expectations to live up to, more phone calls and emails to answer, and if we do not remember to keep slowing ourselves down to focus on "one thing at a time" we become exhausted and stressed. We can adopt the attitude that there are so many choices…so little time! Or we can choose to take things as they come, one activity, one conversation, one task, one moment at a time.

"Action expresses priorities."
- Mahatma Gandhi

The Stinky Cheese says:

- I never have the time to balance my life!
- I need more hours in the day and I can't stand having all of this in my in-box!
- It's terrible how much I have to finish everything.

The Swiss Wiz says:

- Delegate! Know your limits!
- Set boundaries! Prioritize!
- Let go of perfection and realize you can only do so much.

The Swiss Cheese Fairy of Life says:

- This is not a race; slow down and relax!
- Please don't be so hard on yourself—you are special, no matter what!
- You do not have to prove yourself to anyone.

*"The key is not to prioritize what's on your schedule,
but to schedule your priorities."*

– Stephen Covey

Consider the example of a successful professional whose marriage
and relationship with friends has been put on the back burner and
marginalized in the pursuit of success. Or, to a more extreme degree,
the person who is so intent on climbing up the corporate ladder that
they set themselves up for the big fall off the ladder and into marital
estrangement and divorce.

Consider the perfect mom that spends so much emotional energy raising
the perfect children, maintaining the perfect home and doing everything
for everyone. At some point she begins to question her own life, and
perhaps loses her own sense of purpose and confidence, especially if her
perfect kids do not turn out as she had tried to orchestrate.

How about when people neglect friends and hobbies in pursuit of passion
and romance–and when the love is unrequited, there is little to show
for their time spent while their old friends are no longer around? They
end up feeling alone and out of touch with those around them and even
themselves.

In pursuit of money, success, careers, or relationships, it is common for
people to feel that they are experiencing a major life imbalance, and
feel emotionally and physically drained. Focusing too much on goals or
results, or doing too much instead of enjoying the process, results in an
empty feeling.

**Yes, you can have your cheese and eat it, too–as long as you know
how to slice it!**

Focus not only on the product, but in the process, since that is where you
spend most of your time.

Ask the Therapist

Q: I would love to just relax sometimes and read a book, but I feel like I never have time to do that. What can I do to get time for myself without feeling guilty?

A: It is interesting that we do other time-consuming activities like watch TV, shop, talk on the phone, and spend time on the computer without even thinking about how much time we are wasting. Few of us plan to spend one to four hours a day watching TV, surfing the net, talking on the phone, texting, emailing, or shopping, yet we do. Arrange a block of time for yourself. Set aside a half hour a day of uninterrupted time for yourself. You may need to get up earlier in the morning to read, or make a conscious effort to have "me time" after dinner or in the evening. Choose a time when you can go in a private space and read your book. Set a timer so that you are allowing yourself to take a break, and then reconnect with other activities once that time is over. Many people enjoy reading before bedtime, and it might be a nice way to relax and unwind from the day. The main thing to realize is that need to reclaim your time. The good news is that you are actually the master of your time. Even in difficult times, it is important to understand that you need YOU time. Stop feeling guilty and begin to gain control over your choices and lead yourself to a more balanced path. Be flexible with your time, but understand that you will be better to everyone if you replenish yourself. How you manage your time will be the key to feeling centered.

Get a life!

In his book, *Shut Up, Stop Whining and Get a Life,* Larry Winget writes, "You may have tough times. While these tough times are not any fun, there is a lesson to be learned. Enjoy the idea that you are going to be better for having survived the experience…Many times enjoyment comes not by a change in conditions but by a change in awareness. When was the last time you really enjoyed some of the simple things in life? If you want to enjoy your life more, then begin by learning to enjoy the things you take for granted: things you probably do unconsciously everyday… Life is short and getting shorter all the time…Why do you care so much what others think anyway? Who are they to judge you? They are not living your life–you are. Get on with your life and enjoy it."

Anne Wilson Schaef in her book, *Meditations for Women Who Do Too Much,* states, "Just as nature needs balance, people need balance. We need time to be whole persons, and this means balance. We are constantly being drained. Therefore, we need to be fed, and we need time to digest the nourishment. Work and love are better than just work alone and…there is more."

"Teachers open the door, but you must enter by yourself."
— *Ancient Chinese Proverb*

"Life shrinks or expands in proportion to one's courage."
— *Anais Nin*

*"There is more to life than work,
but there is not more to work than life."*
— *Lora Shor*

How do you divide your time?

Are you spending more time on the "have to" rather than the "want to" in your life? Do you feel a sense of flexibility and control over the choices you make or do you feel wedged in a maze of commitments that leave few options for yourself? Think of a specific goal that you would like to accomplish in your quest for balance. A specific goal offers us the mindset that we made a commitment and we are willing to take the steps to break down the goal into tasks that will allow us to accomplish the goal. This will help you learn how to get your slice of the cheese wheel in the way that you want to!

I decided that this would be a great time to have a family meeting. If we see our family as a team, we can really work together for a win-win outcome!

 I really like that idea, let's get the kids involved so we have more time to enjoy activities with them and still have time to be together.

want to
want to

have to
have to

In the words of
The Swiss Wiz...

- Striving for balance is something we can choose to do every day.
- Choosing balance is an on-going process, not a destination.
- Don't forget to recharge yourself, just like you recharge the batteries in your cell phone.
- Ask yourself throughout the day, "What is the best use of my time right now?"
- Prioritize–your slices are not unlimited! You can't do it all—at least not all at the same time!

In the words of
The Swiss Cheese Fairy of Life...

- Joy and happiness are the by-products of leading a balanced life.
- Balance nurtures your body, mind and soul.
- Be gentle with yourself and allow yourself time to relax and take time for you.
- Being flexible will help you accept where you are at...and where you are going.

Swiss Cheese
Tool Kit

Assembling the Metaphorical Tool Kit

The cheese slicer in your metaphorical tool kit serves as a reminder to look at how you slice your time and energy in order to gain or maintain balance in your life.

Ask yourself, what do you value in your life? Are you giving people, things or events that you value in your life their fair share? Although you might know what your values are, do the slices in your life reflect that? If not, then remind yourself that you are able to choose how big or small your slices will be in many areas of your life.

Learn to gain awareness of your day-to-day activities and examine how much time you spend at work, at home and at play! Yes, even adults need time to play, to relax and to decompress. There may be enough time and energy for everything that you need or want to do; it may just take a change of perspective or a change in the way you do things throughout your hours, days and weeks.

Carefully choose and take some time to decide and prioritize how large or small you want your slices to be and how you divide your time and energy, as well as your mental focus. If you devote a large chunk to one area, remember that you will have less for the other pieces. Slice it into too many pieces and there might not be enough time for you.

Balance is all about how you slice it!

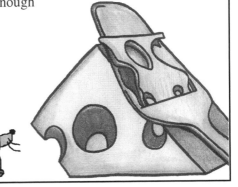

Ninth Slice

Mastering the Cheese Wheel of Change!

How To Be a Stress Manager… Not a Stress Carrier!

Mastering the Cheese Wheel of Change!
How To Be a Stress Manager... Not a Stress Carrier!

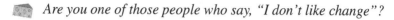 *Are you one of those people who say, "I don't like change"?*

Does change too often cause uncertainty and trigger anxiety?

Do you think time is changing you instead of you changing with the times?

Do you feel your stress level controls you rather than you controlling it?

Do you manage your stress; or do you carry it and give it to others?

There is an old proverb: *Change is the only constant.* Change is a necessary part of everyday life–even in nature, without change, trees decay and flowers do not bloom. If things do not change, life becomes dormant, stuck in limbo–a mere snapshot of its potential. Without transformations in the animal world, the butterfly never emerges from its cocoon and the snake never sheds its skin.

At times, we need to shed old patterns and ways of thinking to make way for new growth and new attitudes. You can also think of change like waves in the ocean–they are all different, somewhat unpredictable, sometimes ebbing in and out gently and other times coming in with a roar. Life is a process of ebbing and flowing, alternating between forcefulness and calmness with all the degrees in between.

The beauty of this process cannot be stopped, neither in the ocean nor in ourselves. By going with the flow, we can also let our beauty unfold, in accordance with our own nature.

The Times They Are a-Changin'

Bob Dylan's well-known song, *The Times They Are a-Changin'*, has touched generations young and old with a message that is as true now as it was over 30 years ago. The theme of the song has proved timeless. As time moves on, lives are transformed, both for the better and for the worse. Life evolves, things change, and circumstances change.

Bob Dylan's timeless lyrics are a comfort to those who may feel trapped in situations beyond their control. Nothing stays stagnant and although you might feel like an underdog at some point in your life, you might at another point come out on top. The song offers hope to those unhappy with their present lot, and a caution to those who see themselves as winners–their lives seem to go on without a hitch. For example, the line "your sons and your daughters are beyond your command" can serve as a basis of analogy to those parents who demand perfection of their honor roll student–viewing a C or even a B as substandard. Parents set themselves up for a huge disappointment if they feel entitled and expect things from their gifted children, who later on might turn out to never quite live up to their potential. Meanwhile, the less gifted child next door might become a high achiever in life, successful both professionally and personally. For the winners and losers, and everyone in between, change cannot be avoided and needs to be embraced. Stay nimble, stay flexible, adjust expectations, and you will stay on top of the tides of change.

"We change, whether we like it or not."
- Ralph Waldo Emerson

"They always say time changes things,
but you actually have to change them yourself."
-Andy Warhol

The National Theme of CHANGE!

One of President Barack Obama's themes for his 2008 presidential campaign was "Change." This theme resonated in the hearts and minds of many Americans. Just as time does not stand still, our lives do not stay stagnant. The more we are flexible, the more we can embrace change, enabling us to grow and evolve.

Q: How many psychologists does it take to change a light bulb?

A: One, but the light bulb has to want to change.

As a therapist, I have seen many clients and patients walk through my office with a large amount of pain or anger. All too often, clients point their finger at others for being the root of their problems, thinking they should change and are indignant that people are just not fair. The problem with this approach is that you can't *make* anyone change and you are not guaranteed a fair life no matter how much you think you deserve it. Really, the only power you have is to change yourself–and even that is hard to do! Change-resistant clients talk about how unhappy or unsatisfying their life situation is, yet they keep on doing the same things and expect different results. To break this vicious cycle, they need to see themselves as agents of change and be the light bulb that wants to change!

There is no constant in life, which is a good thing otherwise one might permanently be stuck in the hole, buried six feet under.

The Swiss Cheese Theory of Life teaches us that although we might be in the hole we can still get out of the hole by making changes.

For some of us, that might mean we need to face our fears, uncertainties, anxieties, trepidations and all the other stinky things around us. When things stink in our lives, it might be time to leave it behind…just like cheese that is past the expiration date. *If something is expired, do you really want to eat it?*

> *"Be the change you wish to see in the world."*
> *- Mahatma Gandhi*

Don't Miss Out on the Opportunities Because of Inflexible Thinking!

The following cartoon gives us a humorous view of a serious, yet common situation. We think we know what is best for us and we are sometimes so sure of what we want that we do not see the potential gifts along the way. Rigid expectations can prevent us from seeing the gifts we get when things do not turn out as planned. It's fine to strive for what you want, but be flexible enough to realize that there could be a variety of good outcomes. Why not try letting go of your absolutes and preconceptions, and accept how things fall into place.

- Getting into your first choice college does not necessarily mean it works out the best.
- If you make it work, the job or college choice that you prefer the least could be the best thing that ever happened to you!
- Feeling great pain after a relationship break-up could be a blessing in disguise, as you might learn more from it than you ever realized!
- Many clients, in retrospect, were so glad they hit rock bottom because that was their impetus to take stock of themselves and begin to really change.

"Opportunity paged me, beeped me, linked me,
e-mailed me, faxed me, and spammed me.
But I was expecting it to knock!"

Are You Like the Blind Swiss?

As stated in the introduction, there is actually a type of Swiss which has no holes–or no "eyes," in official cheese-making terms. Yes, that's right! The holes in the Swiss are technically called eyes. Without the eyes, the Swiss cheese is blind!

You might say that Swiss cheese without eyes is cheese in denial!

Flexibility in thinking requires the ability to give up pre-conceptions and stereotypes and not accept things blindly; simply because that is the way they have always been done.

A mother was making a roast and her daughter asked her why she cut off the ends before putting it into the pan. She responded that her mother had always done it this way. The daughter then went to the grandmother and asked her why she cut off the ends, and her grandmother told her, "The pan I had back then was small, so I had to cut the ends off to fit it in the pan." Sometimes we follow along with what we have always done without thinking for ourselves and seeing whether it still makes sense to do it the same way.

There was a devoutly religious man whose boat was destroyed at sea and he was clinging to a life raft–expecting that God would rescue him since he had always been such a pious man. A helicopter flew over and put a ladder down for him, but the man refused to get in, exclaiming that he was waiting to be rescued by God. A large commercial boat and a smaller sailboat came by, both offering help, and he told them the same thing. Eventually a storm washed him away and he died.

In heaven, when he met his god, he asked why God did not save him. God responded, "I tried to! I sent you a helicopter and two boats and you wouldn't go on any of them!" The man had a preconception of how God was going to appear and ended up missing out on God's help!

> *"There is nothing permanent except change."*
> *– Heraclitus (Greek philosopher, 540-480 BC)*

> *"The definition of insanity is doing the same thing over and over again and expecting different results."*
> *- Einstein*

Are You Like Scaredy Squirrel?

Adults can learn a lot from children's books. Melanie Watt's colorful children's book *Scaredy Squirrel* depicts the ludicrousness of the fear of change. Scaredy Squirrel lives alone in a tree and spends his day eating nuts, looking out of his tree, and protecting himself and his food stash from the unknown. He has a very predictable daily schedule consisting of eating, looking out at the view and sleeping, all in a specific order. He fears most things in the outside world, both real and imagined, including Martians, germs, poison ivy, and sharks. Even though he often feels bored, he is happy that he is safe and weighs the advantages of staying where he is: great view, plenty of nuts, safe place; with the disadvantages of never leaving the tree, i.e., same old view, same old nuts, same old place.

If he ventured out of his tree and found his way to a therapist's office, he could very well be diagnosed with an Obsessive Compulsive Personality style.

Scaredy Squirrel needs to have control over the unknown, makes schedules for himself, and is fearful of what he cannot control. His anxiety is always raised due to the *what-ifs*–he prepared an emergency kit with antibacterial soap, a net to catch insects, and a parachute, among many other items. One day, when a bee stings him in his tree, he leaps out to discover that he is a *flying* squirrel! He never would have realized this if he stayed safe in the tree and did not get the push to venture out! Are you holding yourself back in fear of the unknown, preventing yourself from living life to the fullest?

We, too, have potential to soar, and by playing it safe and resisting change, we end up letting fear prevent us from being free to actualize our potential.

What can you find out about yourself when you do not cling to the same old routine? Can you fly too?

After this experience of jumping into the unknown, Scaredy Squirrel changes his schedule and gives himself exactly seven minutes to jump into the unknown.

What areas of your life are unknown that you would like to jump into? Give yourself more than seven minutes a day!

> *"If I were dying, my last words would be:*
> *Have faith and pursue the unknown end."*
> *– Oliver Wendell Holmes*

Emotional Vampires Have a Hard Time With Change!

Albert Bernstein's *Emotional Vampires* also uses a tongue-in-cheek approach to depict the change-phobic nature of the obsessive personality style. Emotional vampire is the term that Bernstein uses for people who have personality styles that are change-resistant and inflexible. These psychological vampires do not prey on blood, but rather, they suck the energy out of those that cross their path!

This rigid style exemplifies a person who resists change due to fear or anxiety about what is not in their control. Worrying about being proven wrong can lead to distorted fears. In the Scaredy Squirrel story, the dangers lurking in the outside world were magnified beyond what was real. Bernstein writes, "Obsessive-compulsive vampires are the living embodiment of too much of a good thing. In their world, no mistake is insignificant, and all the work is never done." He goes on to say, "Obsessive-compulsive vampires are deathly afraid of doing anything wrong. To them, the smallest crack in their perfect facade leaves them open and vulnerable to all the seeping horrors of the universe."

People with low self-esteem see flexible thinking as proof that what they originally thought was wrong. They avoid re-evaluating, like the plague.

Does that sound like you or someone you know?

Client Example:
I Decided to Be Mad

"I am furious with my sister! She keeps on blowing us off. I don't care about me, but how about my kids? She only does what is convenient for her! We usually get together every year at Thanksgiving and this year they are not even coming!"

Laurie was going to tell her a thing or two when they visited a few weeks later. She was furious, but tried to be pleasant, waiting for the right time to tell her sister how angry she was. Luckily, before she said anything, her sister mentioned that she spent the previous weekend at her 25th high school reunion where she met up with her old friends for the first time in 15 years!

Despite this new knowledge which explained why her sister skipped their annual get-together, Laurie still felt angry because she "didn't want to stop being mad." After talking it over in counseling, she realized the fear of changing her mind would be an admission that she was wrong. She used this realization as an opportunity to learn to let go of preconceived notions and judgments that only fueled her sense of self-righteousness and defensiveness.

The Cheese Only Lasts So Long!

Spencer Johnson's bestseller, *Who Moved My Cheese?* shares our cheesy theme. In his book, Johnson describes four characters who have different approaches to change: two mice, Sniff (sniffs out change) and Scurry (plows ahead without much thought); and two miniature humans, Hem (resists change due to a sense of entitlement and fear of change–which ends up making him feel like a victim) and Haw (who approaches and adjusts to change slowly and methodically).

These characters represent the general ways people react to change, and we all can relate to one, or a combination, of the characters. As Johnson's characters go through a maze in search of a fresh piece of cheese, they realize that they need to let go of expecting the cheese to be in one predictable place. This parable shows that only by embracing change and refusing to hang on to how things are "supposed to be," can one thrive and flourish.

Johnson's mini-humans, Hem and Haw, resist looking for new cheese when the cheese is not where it usually was found. By circumstances out of their control, the cheese was moved. Those characters assumed that new cheese should simply "appear" in the old place, and felt indignant that it was not appearing like it was "supposed to." Consequently, their resistance to change made them the last to find the new cheese so they stayed the hungriest, the longest. In this parable, we are convinced that the characters that are the healthiest are proactive in dealing with change rather than expending energy being angry that things should be predictable and go their way. People often get stuck with the idea that their lives should change in their favor, rather than accept the new conditions and get over it.

Throughout the book, we see Haw's transformation from being fearful and hesitant of change to embracing the need for change. Towards the end of the book, in fact, Haw chisels a message on a wall of the maze to tell his friend, Hem, *"If You Do Not Change, You Can Become Extinct."*

In another symbolic parable about change, *Our Iceberg is Melting: Changing and Succeeding Under Any Conditions,* authors Kotter and Rathgeber use the breakup of an iceberg as a symbol of impending change. The underlying message of this parable is again to stress the importance of adapting to change rather than resisting it. The penguins living on the breaking iceberg that resist change are less likely to survive. In contrast, the penguins that plan, anticipate and embrace change find themselves more equipped to deal with new life circumstances.

"We must always change, renew,
rejuvenate ourselves; otherwise we harden."
- Johann Wolfgang von Goethe

Transformations in Nature

We can learn about the importance, and even the beauty, of change not only through parables, but also in nature. Consider the caterpillar that sheds it skin to emerge into a beautiful butterfly. The butterfly is only capable of flying after shedding its former self and transforming into a newer and more colorful self.

Just think: If the caterpillar was change resistant, there would not be any beautiful butterflies!

The snake sheds its skin to grow. To grow as humans, we need to emerge from a younger version of ourselves to keep on reinventing ourselves as we change and mature. The outer layers of both the caterpillar and the snake change, but some of their essence still remains on the inside despite the outer transformation. A new self emerges based on the foundation of their old self. They reinvent themselves as they actualize their potential.

Every fall, trees shed their leaves, flowers and plants shrivel and die. But next spring, the new growth shows that they did not really die. Blossoms come out in full force from a place that looked stark just weeks before. The trees and plants grow stronger and blossom even more fiercely each year, despite their outward appearance during the winter.

To increase his chances of survival, a chameleon changes colors to blend into the background. If the chameleon stayed the same, he would be less likely to survive. Animals that are more capable of adapting to their surroundings are more likely to survive and thrive!

Nature reveals change and growth in almost every living thing–that is what makes nature so beautiful. Likewise, allow yourself to transform, let new growth appear and shed some of the old habits and ways of thinking that no longer fit with your own personal evolution.

Mini-Exercise

Before stressing over this concept of change, let's try to tie it to stress. Think about how you would finish this phrase:

Stress is _____.

What are the first thoughts that come to your mind?
Write out five to ten responses.

If you are like most people, the majority of the items would have a negative connotation. Common answers include:

Not having enough time
Anxiety
Pressure
Financial trouble
Traffic
Work hassles
Marital problems
In-law problems

People often view stress as negative, as something to be avoided or quickly resolved. However, avoiding stress is like avoiding life.

Don't Avoid Change! Don't Avoid Stress!
Embrace Change and Stress!

Stress researcher, Hans Selye, claimed that "the absence of stress is death." He also said, "stress is the spice of life." This gives the concept of stress a whole new meaning–stress is no longer something to be avoided or feared.

Stress is healthy, as long as you learn to
manage your stress and not carry it!

Activity

Look at the answers you used to finish the phrase "Stress is..." Were there any items that could be viewed as positive? Now that you have learned a new attitude about stress, how about adding some more items? Put a minus sign next to the answers you see as negative and a plus sign next to those items you see as positive. This exercise will remind you that stress is a mixed bag. Remember, there are no right answers because stress is neither good nor bad.

Here are examples of positive stress:

- Playing in the big game.
- Getting married.
- Starting a new job.
- Having a baby.
- Going on an adventure vacation.

Stress just "IS."

Did you know...

stressed spelled backwards is...desserts?
It shows how sweet stress can be!

The Stinky Cheese

is a stress carrier and might be caught saying:

- She shouldn't get so upset!
- Why can't she just chill?
- What's the matter with this world nowa-days?

He also tends to…

- Judge others
- Act impatient and irritable
- Feel isolated
- Be dissatisfied

The Swiss Wiz

knows how to manage stress and says:

- Stress can work for you, rather than against you.
- If you are not afraid of change, you won't be holding yourself back!
- If you are flexible, change is much easier.

and tends to…

- Look at things positively.
- Feel in control without controlling others.
- Feel satisfied.

A Stress Manager has Stress Hardiness Skills!

Psychologist Dr. Suzanne Kobasa depicts four factors of the stress-hardy personality, characterized by emotional resiliency.

Commitment: Those who feel a sense of commitment have a sense of involvement in something outside of themselves. They feel a connection with others and the world around them, and they see their actions as working towards a greater good. They find meaning in their commitments.

Control: Rather than feel a victim of circumstance, or a pawn in the lives of others, stress-hardy people see that they have an internal locus of control. They have a sense of control over their lives, they feel a need to control others, and do not believe that they are at the mercy of others. They abide by the Serenity Prayer by Reinhold Niebuhr: *"God, grant me the serenity to accept the things I cannot change; courage to change the things I can; and wisdom to know the difference."*

Challenge: In the face of adversity, people who are stress-hardy thrive on being challenged without being overwhelmed. They feel empowered to transform adversity into victory. They have confidence in their abilities to rise to the challenge. They do not shy away from change or new situations.

Connection: Stress-hardy people who do not isolate themselves and are open to making and keeping strong connections tend to be happier and more resilient than those who shy away from close connections. Those who tend to keep others at a distance and isolate themselves are often left feeling more depressed, lonely, and anxious.

"Life will bring you to your knees and keep you there. Permanently, if you let it. It's not about how hard you hit.
It's about how hard you can get hit. And keep moving forward. Keep moving forward. If you know what you're worth, go out and get it. But you have to be willing to take the hit."
- Sylvester Stallone in Rocky Balboa

How Do You Get Through the Holes?

The Case for Resiliency

In the process of fermentation in bread, have you ever noticed how the yeast powder becomes foamy and voluminous when mixed with water and, unless watched carefully, it overflows in the dish it is rising in? It's just as important for people to show resiliency by expanding their minds, and being flexible, to avoid staying stagnant.

Did you know that fermentation leads to the sweetness of the Swiss?

That's right! Tasty Swiss arises from bacteria, just as baking bread requires bacteria to ferment so that yeast can multiply. Although fermentation does not seem like a pretty process, anyone who has made bread from scratch knows you need these brown bubbles of bacteria fermenting the yeast to create delectable and light bread. It is the fermentation that leads to sweet and airy bread. Similarly, the more bacteria used in making Swiss, the larger the holes and the sweeter the cheese!

Even Swiss has its dark side!

Through adversity and darkness comes beauty. And it is only though life's challenges, or getting through the holes, that life tastes truly rich like a great piece of tasty Swiss.

Going Through vs. Being Stuck in the Hole

In *The Lord is My Shepherd: Healing Wisdom of the Twenty-third Psalm,* Dr. Harold Kushner has a very interesting observation about King David's widely repeated psalm. A portion of this psalm that is used to comfort mourners reads, *"...though I walk through the valley of the shadow of death, I will fear no evil: for thou art with me."* Kushner makes a point of focusing on one little word: *"through."* He claims the choice of the word *through* suggests that the surviving loved ones do not need to stay *in* the shadows, but rather they can move *through* them. This concept offers hope to the mourner who feels as if life will never be the same after suffering from a loss.

Whether it is losing a loved one or facing the reality that a dream you held so dearly will not come true, those who possess the seeds of emotional resilience do not get stuck *in* the shadow, but go *through* the shadow to the other side.

> *"We could never learn to be brave and patient*
> *if there were only joy in the world."*
> *- Helen Keller*

In the words of
The Swiss Wiz...

- Adapting to change takes a lot of mental flexibility!

- Remember, stress is not good or bad, it just IS!

- Those who embrace change will overcome obstacles and challenges easier than those who resist it.

- We have, within ourselves, the seeds of resilience to keep transforming and growing.

- Don't miss out on opportunities because you expect things to come in certain packages!

In the words of
The Swiss Cheese
Fairy of Life...

- To embrace change means to have faith in your ability to grow.

- You don't need to be scared or afraid.

- Have faith in yourself that you can be resilient!

- Change can be difficult, but it can also be healing and uplifting.

- You don't have to feel alone—I am there with you.

Swiss Cheese Tool Kit

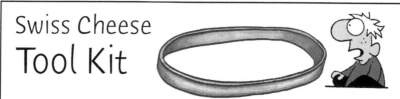

Assembling the Metaphorical Tool Kit

The rubber band in your metaphorical tool kit serves to remind you that some stress in our lives is necessary and good. Stress has been given a bad rap! We usually think of stress as negative, but stress can be positive. If the rubber band did not have any elasticity, it would be limp and lifeless and would not be capable of holding things together and then bouncing back!

Change brings stress, stress leads to change and that is how we grow and flourish. Remember Scaredy Squirrel, who lived his life in complacent boredom due to anxiety about the outside world, including the germs and other menaces? When he finally was forced out of the tree by a bee sting, he learned he could fly and decided to explore the unknown. He became happier as he embraced the unknown.

Are there things that are stopping you because of a fear of the unknown? Are you looking for too much certainty, and thereby, limiting your potential to change?

What are you waiting for? With the visualization of the resilient rubber band, you can:

Stress for Success! Use it to invigorate yourself!

Stretch the elastic enough to give it form and function, but don't pull too hard that it snaps!

Remember the art of balance in being a stress manager.

Tenth Slice

Smile and Say Cheese!

Forgiveness, Gratitude and Optimism

Smile and Say Cheese!
Forgiveness, Gratitude and Optimism

Do you find yourself more bitter than grateful?

Are you so busy that you forget to stop and smell the flowers?

Is your brow furrowed more often than relaxed?

Are you holding onto grudges?

Do you tend to look more at what is going wrong in your life than what is going well?

Happiness is a choice. The more grateful and optimistic we are, the happier we will be, regardless of the curve balls that life throws at us.

Choosing forgiveness and gratitude over bitterness will allow us to smile inside as well as out. Not ready to let go of the thoughts that your boss, kids, family members or an ex-spouse are making your life a living hell? Has a break-up left you feeling bitter and angry? It is important to realize that hanging on to anger hurts you more than it hurts the other person.

The ability to forgive others for perceived wrongdoing is a gift we give to ourselves. That does not mean you condone the disturbing behavior of others, but rather, forgiveness implies that you accept the person for acting poorly due to their own limitations. Forgiveness entails the knowledge and acceptance that people cannot give you what they do not have themselves.

Optimistic thinking can only flourish if you say goodbye to resentment. Give yourself the gifts of optimism and gratefulness! As Nelson Mandela has said, "resentment is like drinking poison and then hoping it will kill your enemies." With an attitude of appreciation, Thanksgiving will not only come around once a year–every day will be Thanksgiving!

What kind of person are you?

It all comes down to whether you choose to be an optimistic or a pessimistic thinker.

Try to surround yourself with positive thinking–negative thinking is contagious, but so is positive!

It's your choice–would you rather spread germs, or love and good will?

Do you tend to look at the whole? Or do you focus on the hole–what's missing?

Are you able to grow from adversity by opening yourself up to the new ways of thinking?

> *"You can't discover light by analyzing darkness."*
> *- Wayne Dyer*

Do you tend to focus on the "hole" - what's missing?

Or Do You Tend to look at the "Whole?"

Ask the Therapist: Is Optimism Really a Choice?

Lora

Q: Do you mean to say that you don't believe that some people are wired to look at things with a more pessimistic outlook? An attitude adjustment can't cure someone who is anxious, depressed or bipolar. What they need is medication.

A: Certainly, as therapists, we are exquisitely sensitive to the help and hope that medication offers to those who experience anxiety, depression and mood imbalances. It is very clear that medications, are often quite helpful. However, medication alone is not the answer. Too often people do not venture into counseling expecting medication to do all the work.

There are also people in therapy who seem resistant even when medication is indicated. Some clients think that taking medication means they are damaged or faulty. We use the following analogies to help them develop a new perspective:

1. Although you can defrost chicken on the countertop, if it is close to dinnertime then popping the frozen chicken in the microwave will certainly fast forward the thawing process and you have a better chance of eating at a decent hour. If you decide to defrost on the countertop, you might get the same result, but it will take a lot longer and you might be eating at bedtime!

2. We also use the analogy of the diabetic. You can certainly try to control your diabetes by eating the right food, but if that alone does not work, very few people would reject the notion of using insulin in addition to help regulate sugar levels.

Choose Happiness NOW!

In his book, *Happiness NOW!*, Robert Holden emphasizes that happiness is a choice and something we can choose *RIGHT NOW!* He laments that most people think there are preconditions to happiness. Thus, the pursuit of happiness actually interferes with our happiness because we are pursuing it instead of looking within ourselves in the *NOW*. The past is past and dwelling on the past prevents you from feeling happiness *NOW!*

In his book, Holden differentiates between two senses of self–the *Unconditioned Self* and the *Conditioned Self*. "The unconditioned self is like the child within us, living in the present without being judgmental. It accepts life as it is, not how it should be or would have been. It represents a self-image that is beautiful and unique. The unconditioned self says, *"I am whole."* In contrast, the conditioned self is comprised of judgments and self-doubts about your essential goodness and worthiness. It harbors self-doubt and criticism. The conditioned self asks, *'Am I whole?'"*

So, do you feel *WHOLE* or are you questioning if you are *WHOLE?*

MAKE YOUR CHOICE! It's all up to you!

> *"Many people mistakenly believe that
> circumstances make a person.
> They don't. Instead,they reveal a person."*
> - *Wayne Dyer*

Client Example:
She Still had Some Life Left

Martha, age 73, had little zest for life after her husband of 42 years died suddenly. The light of her life was her adult children and grandchildren. Aside from family dinners and baby-sitting, she kept to herself. Martha was lonely, but did not know where to turn. Her support system shrunk considerably as many of her friends became ill or died. Despite her sharp mind and able body, she found herself wondering if there was much life left in her. At the urging of her family doctor, she reluctantly came for counseling. It took only one session for her to realize that "there is still life in me." She began to look into activities at the local senior citizen center. At the center, Martha joined a choir and rekindled her love of bridge and started playing the game again for the first time in over 30 years. Through these activities, she met a new group of friends and consequently felt a renewed zeal for living.

*"While we may not be able to control what happens to us,
we can control what happens inside of us."*
- *Benjamin Franklin*

What is an Optimistic Thinker?

First, let's see what it is not!

An optimistic thinker is *NOT* someone who:

- Says they don't care, when they do.
- Says that things are fine, when they're not.
- Shrugs off problems rather than working on them.
- Views setbacks as dead ends.
- Values self-worth based on comparisons with others.

An optimistic thinker *IS* someone who:

- Learns from adversity rather than getting stuck.
- Does not expect perfection.
- Sees things in a positive way.
- Is resilient.
- Lives in the present rather than the past or future.
- Is happy to be alive!

> *"A pessimist finds difficulty in every opportunity; an optimist finds opportunity in every difficulty."*
> - *Unknown*

Benefits to Optimistic Thinking

1. When you think clearly, your relationships flourish.

2. You don't need to look for blame in others.

3. Life is more fun!

4. Grudges and resentments disappear.

5. You have fewer issues.

6. You are more likeable to yourself and others.

7. You are nicer!

8. You listen better without the static.

9. You have more energy!

10. You have a sense of humor!

11. You are more successful in work and in life!

12. You feel empowered.

13. Positive energy emanates!

14. Courage replaces fear.

15. You like to laugh!

"If you don't like something, change it.
If you can't change it, change your attitude."
- Maya Angelou

The Swiss Cheese Fairy of Life says:

Happiness is…

…being in the hole, but realizing that the sun is still shining. The shade from being in the hole can protect you from the harmful rays of the sun. The hole can be a time of reflection, so you don't get burned!

We all know people that have a sunny disposition and a cheery view of life. We also know others that constantly struggle and are plagued by what is going wrong with their lives, rather than focus on what is going right. Are you one of those strugglers? Are you in the *hole?* Why not choose happiness for a minute, an hour, or even a day? Give yourself a break from those plaguing thoughts–take a mini-vacation.

Even if it is a cloudy day, always remember the sun is still shining above the clouds!

The Stinky Cheese says:

Did you ever hear the expression "happy as a clam"? Has anyone ever seen a happy clam? The ones I know tend to "clam up"!

"A butterfly is a caterpillar with a positive attitude!"

"Most fears cannot withstand the test of careful scrutiny and analysis. When we expose our fears to the light of thoughtful examination they usually just evaporate."

- *Jack Canfield*

Attitude is Everything!

In his colorful and delightful book entitled, *Little Gold Book of YES! Attitude: How to Find, Build and Keep a YES! Attitude for a Lifetime of SUCCESS,* Jeffrey Gitomer claims that a *Yes! Attitude* is a powerful form of a positive attitude where you replace the word *No* in your habitual self-talk with *Yes!*

What is the key to developing this *Yes! Attitude?*

Gitomer suggests committing yourself to at least 15 minutes at the start of your day to reading a book that focuses on positive thinking. Then set aside a few hours each week for additional reading to boost your attitude and help make it stick! He also suggests regularly watching inspirational movies for an attitude boost. Gitomer shares a time in his life when he personally watched the same movie over and over again, *Challenge to America,* day after day, so that the inspirational message of the movie would sink in.

He claims that his friends thought he was losing his mind, but this immersion helped him make a shift to positive thinking–and it stuck!

"People are attracted to others (or not) based on attitude, and positive attitude is contagious; you can give it to others.

Positive attitude is the foundation for everything.

- It's the mood you're in when you wake up in the morning.
- It's the mood you're in when you walk into the bathroom in the morning and look in the mirror."

- Jeff Gitomer, *Little Gold Book of YES! Attitude*

Client Example:
Giving Up Preconditions to Happiness

During his first counseling session, 34-year-old Dan told me that he sought help after he could no longer deny the feeling that he was perpetually dissatisfied with his life. He came to the painful realization that unless he changed his attitude, he would not feel better.

"When I was young, I thought, 'When I leave home and go to college, then I'll be happy.' Then when I was in college, I thought, 'I would be happier after I graduated.' Then it was 'when I find love, then I'd be happy.' Then it was 'when I get married and have children, then I would be really happy.' Then it was getting a great job that gave me the promise of happiness. But all these things never really gave me happiness that lasted very long after the initial excitement wore off. At this point I have faced the realization that wherever I go I bring myself, and that self is not a contented person. I am coming for help so I can be happy not then, but *NOW!*"

Dan learned strategies to limit the amount of time he spent on negative thoughts. He gave up the long-standing theory that there are pre-conditions to happiness. He made happiness a choice, and became more proactive in making his life happy rather than waiting for events to shape his attitude. He took charge of his attitude and made the shift to positive thinking.

Yes, sometimes in life we need to shift gears, or make u-turns if we are going in the wrong direction. It's time to cut your losses and waste no more time!

Speaker/Psychologist Bill O'Hanlon tells his audiences that people are not good predictors of what will make them happy. He claims that research has shown that of the things out there that we think will make us happy will only give us short lived happiness at first, but does not help our overall "set point" of happiness. This set point is more likely to be controlled by factors within ourselves, like our attitude.

"Attitude is your choice, not your circumstance."
–Jeffrey Gitomer

As Paulie told Rocky, in the movie "Rocky Balboa," who was struggling with the loss of his wife, "You got to change the channel, Rocky...It's getting depressing!"

Learning Optimism is a Gift to Others!

A positive attitude affects not only you, it is also about everyone around you. The more positive you are, the less you impose unreasonable expectations on others, and the more supportive and even loving you can be.

How can you free yourself at your own negative thinking?

Psychologist/author Richard Carlson suggests writing yourself a nasty letter, pinpointing the negative thoughts you have about yourself, and then challenge them.

Martin Seligman, often referred to as the father of Positive Psychology, wrote a book titled *Learned Optimism: How to Change your Mind and Change your Life.* In this book, which laid the foundation for the field of Positive Psychology, he offers tips to shift from a pessimistic to an optimistic mindset simply by changing one's internal self-talk.

By learning healthier thought habits, one can turn their thinking style from negative to positive. This relatively new theory of Positive Psychology focuses on strengths as keys to happiness rather than focusing on what is wrong or missing.

"As a pessimist, it's always wet weather in the soul, they don't do as well at work, and they get colds that will last all winter. They find themselves failing in crucial situations and their relationships go sour very easily. So when people have those kinds of hurts, if they can find that there is something useful in positive psychology, that's where people start."

- Dr. Martin Seligman in an interview in EQ Today

Shifting Gears to Move Towards Happiness

Client Example:
She Learned She Had Choices

Debbie came into my office tearful; discussing how things in her life never seem to work out.

She said she felt hopeless and wondered why she should think that something could change for her when everything she tried never seemed to lead to anything positive. "I just don't feel hopeful about anything. Things just keep on going wrong."

In counseling, Debbie made a conscious effort to stop focusing on what was wrong. She made a list of what she was passionate about and the first item on her list was her love of animals, which stemmed from her desire to become a vet. She was able to see that if she could break down her large goal of wanting to be a veterinarian into small steps, she could actually accomplish her goal.

She started working with a veterinarian who saw the pride and dedication she had in her work. Debbie's positive attitude and optimism came alive, and her enthusiasm was evident to everyone around her. She was able to take classes part-time and work in the animal hospital. She finished all the requirements for applying to veterinary school, and she was accepted. Debbie realized that so much of what was holding her back was her Debbie Downer attitude. She focused on maintaining a can-do attitude and began to really appreciate all that she had. Debbie's gratitude led to more optimism which allowed her to actually go out and find a fulfilling career.

It doesn't matter where you start from; feeling better about your future allows you to make the changes that you need to in order to enhance your life today. By not dwelling on the negative and by believing that she was in control of her happiness, Debbie set herself free.

Choose an Attitude of Gratitude

The expectation that life should be fair would be nice if true, but that is fiction and not fact.

Instead of wanting events to be a "dream come true," look for ways to feel gratitude with what you have.

Be grateful for the chance to improve on past imperfections to overcome setbacks. Kick the habit of needing pre-conditions to happiness! How about trying an attitude of gratitude!

News Flash! Extra! Extra!

The Keys to Happiness are:

- Acceptance
- Gratitude
- Optimism

Q: Ask the Therapist

A: How can I forgive someone who has hurt me?

With my clients, I often give them the following simple visualization to help them understand how to forgive. I ask them to look at the door in my office, and then I point to the chair beside it. I explain that no matter how much you want that door to be a chair, it's not going to happen. Similarly, when people are a certain way, even though you think that people should not be like that, it does not mean that they will be any different from what they are. I do believe, in general, that people do the best they can with what they have. This does not mean you accept abusive behavior, and certainly it is important to set limits and at times distance yourself from a person who is toxic—and even sever the relationship. The more you can work on forgiving the person for being unhealthy, the less you will be pulled down by it. Expecting them to be something that they are not, you will be the one that ends up hurting the most. As in the example I use in my office, it is like expecting a door to be able to transform into a chair because we think it should be that way! It's just not going to happen!

Forgive...Anyway

The poem below was written on the wall in Mother Theresa's Calcutta orphanage. It highlights the importance of forgiveness as a necessary ingredient to peace and happiness. Holding grudges and being unforgiving will make it impossible to feel a deep sense of gratitude and contentment.

Anyway

*People are often unreasonable, illogical, and
self-centered;
Forgive them anyway.
If you are kind, people may accuse you of selfish,
ulterior motives;
Be kind anyway.
If you are successful, you will win some false friends
and some true enemies;
Succeed anyway.
If you are honest and frank, people may cheat you;
Be honest and frank anyway.
What you spend years building, someone could destroy overnight;
Build anyway.
If you find serenity and happiness, they may be jealous;
Be happy anyway.
The good you do today, people will often forget tomorrow;
Do good anyway.
Give the world the best you have, and it may never be enough;
Give the best you've got anyway.
You see, in the final analysis, it is between you and God;
It was never between you and them anyway.*

- Mother Teresa

The Swiss Wiz cautions:

Optimism does not happen in a vacuum–the closeness and quality of your interpersonal relationships correlates directly with your ability to have a positive attitude.

People change not just through ideas and knowledge, but from relationships.

When you are optimistic you become strong and are less likely to be guided by fear and uncertainty. You put trust in others, with an underlying faith in yourself. Healthy, optimistic people are able to form deep relationships, without the fear of losing themselves. Psychologist Abraham Maslow's famous pyramid of the "hierarchy of needs" emphasizes that the basic needs for physical comfort and a sense of belonging and connection underlies the ability to achieve self-esteem. Connection is a necessary foundation to liking yourself more.

In the words of

The Swiss Wiz...

- Optimism is a choice; it is the foundation of resilience.

- Optimism takes practice and intention.

- Gratefulness and forgiveness are the cornerstones to optimism.

- Living in the present–accepting what "is" offers inner peace and the keys to a happy life!

In the words of

The Swiss Cheese Fairy of Life...

- Don't be too hard on yourself, let light come in!

- We all start at different places. Where you are now is the best place to start.

- I love you just the way you are!

- Don't forget to laugh–it is good for the soul!

- When your heart opens, your mind opens, too!

Swiss Cheese
Tool Kit

Assembling the Metaphorical Tool Kit

In this last chapter, we have chosen the common image of the smiley face to represent happiness and optimism. Add a smiley sticker with this bright yellow happy face to your Swiss Cheese Tool Kit!

We appreciate that life can be challenging, and at times you might feel trapped in a hole with no way out. We hope that this simple image of optimism will serve as a reminder and help you realize that happiness is always within your grasp.

Once you choose to look at your life with more gratitude and optimism, life will get simpler!

Try to go through life with a *half smile*. Psychologists have found that even by consciously upturning your lips slightly and relaxing your face, you can actually help yourself feel more smiley on the inside too!

What will happen if you adopt the habit of a half smile and increase your sense of optimism and gratitude? You will:

- Have more spring in your step!
- Be more likely to enjoy the present moment.
- Be more forgiving.
- Laugh more.
- Express and show your love more.
- Lose interest in judging others.
- Worry and fret less.
- Gain more appreciation for life.
- Acquire a sense of inner peace!

Smile and Say CHEESE!

An Extra Slice

You Can't Miss
With the Swiss!

Final Words From Our Guides

Remember to pack your Tool Kit!

- *Do you want to give The Swiss Cheese Theory of Life a try—not just halfway, but a full 100 percent?*

- *What thoughts, feelings or behaviors, in you, are most like The Swiss Wiz, The Swiss Cheese Fairy or The Stinky Cheese?*

- *Which of the slices are the easiest for you to digest? Which slice is the hardest to incorporate in your life?*

- *How can you use the ten slices of The Swiss Cheese Theory of Life to help you taste how truly delicious life can be?*

Do not let the playfulness of this book fool you. Despite the light manner in which we served up our ten slices, this is serious stuff! These simple, yet profound truths can provide the blueprint for personal balance, healing, and healthy living.

We invite you to keep your Swiss Cheese Tool Kit handy to help you navigate the holes in your life. Consider it a survival kit to help you emerge from life's holes!

As we summarize our ten slices, we can use the ten items that we have assembled throughout the book to remind us of the important lessons of *The Swiss Cheese Theory of Life*. Take a chance and trust yourself, so you can develop the resiliency to grow and thrive no matter what comes your way. Know that The Swiss Cheese Fairy of Life and The Swiss Wiz are always inside of you, guiding you with eagerness and hope!

Swiss Cheese
Tool Kit

Assembling the Metaphorical Tool Kit

Figuratively speaking, we now have our Swiss Cheese Tool Kit all assembled and ready to go! You might choose to leave this bag of symbolic tidbits in a place in the deep recesses of your mind, to pull into your consciousness only in times of need. Or you might keep it in the forefront of your mind to remain focused on the ten vital slices of *The Swiss Cheese Theory of Life*. Whatever your needs are, this tool kit can serve up the reminders you need for a healthy and balanced life!

Let's take stock of our Swiss Cheese Theory of Life Metaphorical Tool Kit

First Slice:
Fondue Can Never Turn Back Into a Block of Cheese

Once the coin is tossed and comes up either heads or tails it cannot be changed. This is a simple example of a counterfactual. Wishing it were tails after it turned up heads is a waste of time. Not all the worrying and wishing in the world will change the facts. Change what you can change, but learn to accept and make peace with what you can't!

Second Slice:
There's No Such Thing as a Perfect Slice of Cheese!

Give yourself the gift of an eraser. We have erasers because we all make mistakes. If there were no mistakes, there would be no erasers! Where did we get this notion that we had to be better than who we are? Try your best, but do not judge yourself against an unrealistic standard. Love yourself despite the mistakes, smudges and all!

Third Slice: No Whine With the Cheese, Please!

Look behind the scenes and be a thought
detective! This magnifying glass will help you
examine your thoughts and those of others.
Irrational thoughts bring on immobilizing feelings
and unhealthy behavior. By examining your
thoughts, you can replace irrational thoughts
with more rational ones, and you'll think more clearly and feel
empowered!

Fourth Slice: If the Cheese is Ripe, Dig In!

We use the image of the soldier to show bravery
and discipline; "soldier on" and *DO SOMETHING!*
Being proactive instead of reactive will give you the
opportunity to make a change in yourself and even
in the world. Pursuing your ideals and your dreams
with a sense of commitment brings a sense of meaning and purpose.
Soldiers are known for their bravery–you can be brave, too! Don't let
fear, or a lack of confidence in your abilities, hold you back!

Fifth Slice: Living Whole Despite the Holes!

Do not underestimate the importance of
spirituality and living in the moment. All too
often, our time is spent anchored to yesterday or
worrying and planning for tomorrow. Both the
past and the future are important in our lives,
but all too often, these two facets of our lives rob us of *NOW!* This
ribbon will symbolize to you that today is a gift–that's why they call
it the *PRESENT!*

Sixth Slice: Enjoy the Wine and Cheese Party!

There are a lot of fun card games we can play
with others and, in most cases, we need at least
one entire deck to play. Likewise, we need people
to play out our hand in life! We can't stand alone!
There are many cards in the deck; sure, some seem better than

others, like the ace or king, but we need them all to play a game. The deck of cards reminds us that we need all types of people in this world and we need to stick together to make a full deck! By the way, don't throw out the Joker! It might be a little careless and wild, but it stands a little outside of the deck and reminds us not to take ourselves too seriously!

Seventh Slice: Cheese Lite!

How about a little bottle of bubbles to play with! Be a kid again! Move around, dance, run, jump, and skip! Be active with regular exercise and healthier eating habits. It will make you feel lighter and more playful, like the bubbles that you make! Watch the bubble reveal the colors of the rainbow while it drifts, as you breathe life into yourself by having fun, lightening up and learning to get active. Take care of *YOU! Lighten up! Get that pep in your step!*

Eighth Slice:
The Cheese Wheel of Life - How Do You Slice It?

What do you value in your life? How do you prioritize? How do you divide your time? Are you working to live or are you living to work? Are you a *human doing* or a *human being?* Are you spending more time in one area of your life that you would like to change? Maybe you are working too much or perhaps you want to buckle down and work more! Ask yourself: Do I leave enough time for friends, family, and *myself?* This cheese slicer reminds you that you can slice your life the way you want!

Ninth Slice: Mastering the Cheese Wheel of Change!

Some people say they do not like change. But without change, how would we grow? We need change in our lives to flourish. Change may bring stress, but remember that stress has been given a *bad rap.* Stress is not bad or good: It just *IS!* We use the rubber band to symbolize how we need enough tension in our lives to feel alive and resilient, but if stretched too much it will snap, and if not stretched at all, it remains limp and lifeless.

In mastering the wheel of change, learn to be a *stress manager* and not a *stress carrier,* who discharges stress by giving it to others!

Tenth Slice: Smile and Say Cheese!

Remember the importance of attitude in daily living. It is not events that define us, it is our attitude. If we choose to look at things with optimism rather than pessimism, we will feel better and more in control. This smiley face, whether it is a ball, a sticker or another novelty item, serves as an unconditional support to us. It reminds us to half smile throughout the day instead of wearing a frown or a long "sad sack" face. People will want to hang out with you more! The more grateful you are, the more grateful they will be to be in your presence!

Is there anything you want to put in your tool kit that has special meaning for you? This is the time! There's plenty of room for more tidbits!

The Stinky Cheese thinks pessimism is realism.

The Stinky Cheese feels like:

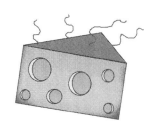

Damaged Goods

A Cracked Egg

A Loser

The Swiss Wiz reminds you to:

Think in rational ways.

Stop exaggerating.

Stop blowing things out of proportion.

Stop weighing yourself down with unhealthy ways of thinking that keep you in a hole.

For those who are weighed down by old patterns, he acknowledges that you can't change the past. However, he emphasizes that what matters is NOW and urges you to rethink things so you can change your take on the past and create a new today.

The Swiss Cheese Fairy feels only love.

She is the beauty inside of you. She is self-love. Just as Dorothy and her friends in the *Wizard of Oz* found what they needed inside of themselves, you can too. She reminds you that every day is a new beginning. In her words: *It's not too late to have a new beginning!*

Make Way for Baby Swiss

This book would not be complete without leaving you with the image of Baby Swiss.

The image of Baby Swiss represents hope, renewed growth, and optimism. With the tools learned from this book, give yourself a chance for a new beginning.

Replace those Stinky Cheese thoughts and behavior with ones that are healthier, gentler and more optimistic. A stinky cheese mentality can only take you so far.

The Stinky Cheese has a short shelf life and it's past its expiration date. Imagine the shelf in your mind being cleared for a new image; that of the Baby Swiss. Fill your head with the optimism, hopefulness and the wonder of Baby Swiss to replace The Stinky Cheese for a fresh start!

Let Baby Swiss be your guide!

Baby Swiss is the child in all of us, the child who needs warmth, support and unconditional love.

Baby Swiss does not do well with harshness or criticism. Teach Baby Swiss with love and compassion.

Take care of Baby Swiss. Hold, cradle and love this beautiful, newly-formed slice of life, because this Baby Swiss lies all around you and inside of you. It is the inner child that needs compassion and love.

Baby Swiss starts fresh on a journey with hope and optimism.

With enthusiasm and hope for a new tomorrow, and an expiration date far in the future, Baby Swiss can bring new life to the world, and to *YOU!*

Each Day is a Chance to Start Anew!

Bibliography

Adams, J. (2003). *When Our Grown Kids Disappoint Us: Letting Go of Their Problems, Loving Them Anyway, and Getting of with Our Lives.* New York: Free Press.

Antony, M. M., & Swinson, R. P. (2009). *When Perfect Isn't Good Enough: Strategies for Coping With Perfectionism.* Oakland, CA: New Harbinger Publications, Inc.

Baum, L. F., & Denslow, W. (1900). *The Wonderful Wizard of Oz.* Chicago: George M. Hill Company.

Belmont, J. A. (2006). *103 Group Activities and Tips.* Eau Claire, WI: PESI.

Belmont, J. A. (2006). *86 Tips for the Therapeutic Toolbox.* Eau Claire, WI: PESI.

Bernstein, A. (2001). *Emotional Vampires: Dealing With People Who Drain You Dry.* New York: McGraw-Hill.

Colbert, D. (2009). *Eat This and Live!* Lake Mary, FL: Siloam.

Coleman, J. (2008). *When Parents Hurt: Compassionate Strategies When You and Your Grown Child Don't Get Along* . New York: HarperCollins Publishers.

Covey, S. R. (1989). *Seven Habits of Highly Effective People.* New York: Free Press.

Dass, R. (1971). *Remember, Be Here Now.* San Cristobal, New Mexico: Hanuman Foundation.

Dodd, P., & Sundheim, D. (2005-2009). *The 25 Best Time Managemnet Tools & Techniques: How to Get More Done Without Driving Yourself Crazy.* Chelsea, MI: Peak Performance Press, Inc.

Dyer, W. (2007). *Change Your Thoughts-Change Your Life: Living the Wisdom of the Tao.* Carlsbad, CA: Hay House.

Dylan, B. (Composer). (1964). *The Times They Are a-Changin'.* [B. Dylan, Performer] On The Times They Are a-Changin'.

Frankl, V. E. (1959). *Man's Search for Meaning.* Boston: Beacon Press.

Freeman, A., & DeWolf, R. (1989). *Woulda, Coulda, Shoulda: Overcoming Regrets, Mistakes, and Missed Opportunities*. New York: HarperCollins Publishers.

Gitomer, J. (2006). *Little Gold Book of YES! Attitude: How to Find, Build and Keep a YES! Attitude for a Lifetime of SUCCESS*. Upper Saddle River, New Jersey: Pearson Education, FT Press.

Glovinsky, C. (2004). *One Thing at a Time: 100 Simple Ways to Live Clutter-Free Every Day*. New York: St. Martin's Press.

Holden, R. (1998). *Happiness Now!: Timeless Wisdom for Feeling Good FAST*. Carlsbad, CA: Hay House.

Johnson, S. (1998). *Who Moved My Cheese?* New York: G.P. Putnam's Sons.

Kabat-Zinn, J. (1994). *Wherever You Go, There You Are*. New York: Hyperion.

Kotter, J., & Rathgeber, H. (2005). *Our Iceberg Is Melting: Changing and Succeeding Under Any Conditions*. New York: St. Martin's Press.

Kushner, H. S. (1996). *How Good Do We Have to Be?: A New Understanding of Guilt and Forgiveness*. Boston: Little, Brown and Company.

Kushner, H. S. (2006). *Overcoming Life's Disappointments*. New York: Random House, Inc.

Kushner, H. S. (2003). *The Lord Is My Shephard: Healing Wisdom of the Twenty-third Psalm*. New York: Anchor Books.

Lakein, A. (1973). *How to Get Control of Your Time and Your Life*. New York: Signet.

Leeds, R. (2008). *One Year to an Organized Life*. Cambridge, MA: Da Capo Press.

Mallinger, A. E., & De Wyze, J. (1992). *Too Perfect: When Being in Control Gets Out of Control*. New York: Random House, Inc.

Morgenstern, J. (2004). *Never Check E-Mail in the Morning*. New York: Fireside.

Morgenstern, J. (2000). *Time Management from the Inside Out*. New York: Henry Holt and Company, LLC.

Niven, D. (2006). *100 Simple Secrets of Happy People: What Scientists Have Learned and How You Can Use It*. New York: HarperCollins Publishers.

Roese, N. (2005). *If Only: How to Turn Regret into Opportunity*. New York: Broadway Books.

Roizen, M. F., & Oz, M. C. (2008). *You: Being Beautiful: The Owner's Manual to Inner and Outer Beauty*. New York: Free Press.

Seligman, M. E. (1990). *Learned Optimism: How to Change your Mind and Change your Life*. New York: Pocket Books.

Seuss, D. (1937). *And to Think That I Saw It on Mulberry Street*. New York: Vanguard Press.

Styne, J., & Merrill, B. (Composers). (1964). People. [B. Streisand, Performer] On *People*.

Twerski, A. (2007). *Happiness and the Human Spirit: The Spirituality of Becoming the Best You Can Be*. Woodstock, VT: Jewish Lights Publishing.

Watt, M. (2006). *Scaredy Squirrel*. Kids Can Press, Ltd.

Williams, M., Teasdale, J., Segal, Z., & Kabat-Zinn, J. (2007). *The Mindful Way through Depression: Freeing Yourself from Chronic Unhappiness*. New York: The Guilford Press.

Wilson Schaef, A. (2004). *Meditations for Women Who Do Too Much*. New York: HarperCollins.

Winget, L. (2004). *Shut Up, Stop Whining and Get a Life*. Hoboken, New Jersey: John Wiley & Sons, Inc.